D1756109

THINKING OF E
A COUNSELLOR?

Jonathan Ingrams

KARNAC

First published in 2012 by
Karnac Books Ltd
118 Finchley Road
London NW3 5HT

ISBN-13: 978-1-78049-016-8

Typeset by Vikatan Publishing Solutions (P) Ltd., Chennai,
India

Printed in Great Britain

www.karnacbooks.com

THINKING OF BECOMING A COUNSELLOR?

CONTENTS

ABOUT THE AUTHOR

Jonathan Ingrams came to counselling following twenty-five years of making medical educational programmes for doctors and general audiences in the United States and Europe. Over the past fourteen years he has practised as a psychotherapist with a broad spectrum of clients from the "worried well" to those suffering a range of mental illnesses of varying severity. His work has included counselling for Young Offenders and taking referrals from GPs, insurance companies, and Employee Assistance Programmes. He is the author of *Counselling ...? Me?: A Guide to the Talking Therapies* (Karnac, 2011).

To Angela

INTRODUCTION

If you've picked up this book it may be that you're thinking of training to be a counsellor. You have perhaps had to raise a family, deal with career changes, cope with grief, with disappointment, with living under financial hardship, or with going through a mid-life crisis. Having survived all of this, it is not unreasonable to wonder whether you could use your range of life experiences in a productive way. The idea of offering comfort and support to someone who is undergoing difficulties you may yourself have gone through and overcome seems to make sense, and indeed is why counselling is one of the few careers where older age can actually be an advantage.

First, we should ask: Is there a need for counselling?

According to the Office for National Statistics (ONS), three out of ten of us experience some kind of psychological difficulty in the course of a year. About 10% of children and one in four unemployed people have a mental health problem at any one time, and the UK has one of the highest rates of self-harm in Europe. The *Journal of Health Economics* (2008, 2010) suggests that depression and mental illness will increase as millions struggle to cope with debts and money problems during the economic downturn.

The British Association for Counselling & Psychotherapy (BACP), a leading authority in the UK, carried out a survey that indicates that the stigma once attached to counselling is disappearing, with 94% of people now considering it acceptable to have psychotherapy for anxiety or depression. The number of people seeking help to cope with divorce or the breakdown of a relationship has increased from 52% to 85% over the past six years.[1] So it is probably fair to say that there is a need for counsellors.

All right, so what exactly is counselling? BACP describes the process as follows:

> "A counselling session is a time set aside in a private, safe place where you and the therapist can talk in confidence about matters that may be troubling you. These may include feelings and emotions about life events or relationships, ways of thinking and patterns of behaviour."

This seems straightforward enough. But then:

> "The therapist will do their best to help you look at your issues and identify the right course of action for you, either to help you resolve your difficulties or find ways of coping. Talking about these things may take time."[2]

Now it gets more complex. Phrases such as "the therapist will do their best to help you look at your issues", "find ways of coping", and "these things may take time" acknowledge that any objectives set will not be easy to define or simple to attain.

This raises a series of questions. What are the criteria for mental well-being? What are the factors that bring about psychological distress? How are these factors identified? And how might an individual coming for counselling be enabled to deal with them?

As you can imagine, much of psychotherapy is about skills in interpretation. Counsellors look beyond the presented facts to understand what might be going on behind the scenes. This requires skills in drawing people out, helping them feel at ease, choosing a style of language that they're comfortable with and, in particular, developing the ability to truly see things from their standpoint.

For over a century and a half the keenest minds have laboured over finding a reliable entry point to the human psyche and the means of understanding it, particularly where mental health is concerned. There has been much disagreement among the experts over the years about how therapy should be practised, often with bickering, argument, and sometimes ruthless backstabbing on a scale as vigorous as any politicking. But equally, many approaches that initially may seem to be entirely divorced from one another can be seen, in hindsight, to share a common philosophy of helping the client get better and stay better.

Socrates said: "The unexamined life is not worth living." So before committing to a counselling course one needs to ask certain questions: What is my philosophy in life? What are my values? What changes in outlook have I experienced or that may be ongoing? How well do I really know myself? You may recognize that you have certain characteristics, but how did you arrive at this conclusion? And how well does it stand up in practice?

This is where you can ask yourself where you think your skills may best lie.

Are they in listening, in dissecting, in analysing? Are you a storyteller? Are you able to help someone see the humorous side of a situation in which they may be involved? How well do you think you may be able to step into someone else's shoes and see life, with its problems and difficulties, as they do?

It is clearly essential for us to have some insight into the impact of events in our childhood and in later years—of skills hard won and lessons learned. As Carl Jung, one of the pioneers of psychotherapy, observed in *Memories, Dreams, Reflections*:

> "The doctor is effective
> only when he himself is affected ...
> Only the wounded physician heals."

The purpose of this book is to try to provide you, the prospective counsellor, with the information you may need to help you decide whether you could be suited to a career in counselling and, if so, what kind of modality might best fit your skills and temperament.

As we will see, the approaches taken by the pioneers of counselling were strongly influenced by their backgrounds, their temperament, and the social climate in which they practised. If you have had a career in a caring profession such as nursing or teaching, your life skills may be different than if you've been running a company or practising as an accountant. You may be more comfortable working with young people or older, with children or adults. The important point is that you do not have to be a particular type of person to make an effective counsellor.

Another major factor influencing the way we see the world is the prevailing culture—the particular language, traditions, ethics, and morals currently predominating. Not so long ago, a man who did not marry was simply seen as a bachelor. Now an unmarried man may often be presumed to have homosexual leanings. (On the other hand, male and female homosexuality is now much more accepted.) Young children used to be able to run free and play without supervision. This is far less likely now.

All of the above notwithstanding, do not try to pin down "normality". As Robert Owen said to colleague William Allen in 1828: "All the world is queer, save thee and me, And even thou art a little queer ..."

* * *

I had better tell you at this point what this book does not set out to do. It is not a how-to manual on the techniques of counselling and psychotherapy. You'll get that if, or when, you start your studies. Nor is it a full account of all the psychological theories and their practitioners. It is designed to give you an insight into the way that the founders of psychotherapy set about addressing their clients' problems, the factors influencing their thinking, and what their approaches set out to achieve. I hope this will enable you to decide whether counselling might be right for you, and if so what kind of method might best harmonize with your temperament.

This is important, not least because if you go ahead you will be spending at least three years in quite intensive training and study at a cost of some £10,000 to £15,000 to achieve the diploma, which is usually the minimum requirement for a counsellor to operate professionally.

This is not an academic work, so there are few references. However, there are useful and understandable books on all aspects of psychotherapy. I have made recommendations at intervals of those you might find it particularly helpful to read as a part of your decision-making process.

So, if you are minded to find out more, which I hope you are, then on to Chapter One.

Notes

1. (2010). *Therapy Today* (2010). One in five Britons has consulted a counselor or psychotherapist. *Volume 21, Issue 7*, p. 5.
2. O'Driscoll, P. (2008). What are counselling and psychotherapy? *BACP Information Sheet*. C2.

Beginnings

It seems only right that we start with Sigmund Freud (1856–1939), the Big Bang from which all psychotherapy emerged. He'll almost certainly be the first authority you'll be introduced to if you go on a counselling course. But although a huge influence on the development of psychotherapy, he didn't emerge from a vacuum, or practice in isolation. Before Freud, superstition and magic were often believed to be the prime controllers of mental functions. A contemporary of Freud, William Walter Atkinson (1862–1932), in his book *Mind and Body or Mental States and Physical Conditions,* published in 1910, observed: "Mental Healing operates under a thousand names, forms and theories in every race, nation and clime in all ages past and present".[1] This remains true to this day. Proof of this can be found in an incident as recently as 2007 in which the actress Phyllida Law had two gargoyles stolen from her garden. She erected a notice warning that she had put a hex on the culprit. Some time later, the statues were returned, with a note from the thief pleading her to lift the curse as he had been very ill since he stole the gargoyles. Law duly put up another notice: "Thank you for returning the statues. All curses lifted."[2]

I leave it to you to decide what was going on here!

The manipulation of the human mind has, of course, been exploited since time immemorial by witch doctors, shamans, and various faith healers practising their art. In the Middle Ages, Edward the Confessor instituted the Royal Touch, a laying on of hands which was believed to cure scrofula, a disfiguring form of tuberculosis known as the "king's evil". (The fact that every supplicant received a gold coin may have encouraged people to present for the cure!) There was even a service laid out in the *Book of Common Prayer* to accompany the process. Although the practice was abandoned in England after the death of Queen Anne in 1714, it continued sporadically in France for a further hundred years.

Next up to the stand is Franz Anton Mesmer (1734–1815). Mesmer developed the concept of "animal magnetism". He claimed that a powerful magnetic field surrounded the body, which, if disturbed or broken, resulted in the person becoming ill. If this "field" were to be repaired or rebalanced, however, then good health could be restored. Mesmer achieved this by touching his clients with an iron rod so that beneficial magnetism flowed into them, and also by "mesmerizing" his clients—that is, looking into their eyes and performing passes up and down their arms.

The huge success of this venture later encouraged him to treat his patients en masse by seating groups of them in a large wooden tub in which bottles of "magnetized" water, resting on a bed of iron filings, were placed at strategic intervals radiating from the centre. The tub had holes in it through which jointed iron rods were placed. Mesmer would instruct assistants to direct the iron rods to different parts of the participants' anatomies. Unsurprisingly, in this heady atmosphere, his patients would sometimes exhibit signs of hysteria or undergo convulsions. The king of France offered Mesmer a large sum of money if he would publish his secret, but Mesmer (wisely) refused.

For all they might look like music hall acts, it is sobering to recognize that interventions like the Royal Touch and mesmerism could not have gone on as long as they did without getting results. Many thousands put themselves forward for treatment and, indeed, mesmerism continued to be practised after the death of its originator.

It is unlikely, if you take up counselling training, that you'll be introduced to the philosophy of a watchmaker with an enquiring mind rejoicing under the name of Phineas Parkhurst Quimby (1802–1866), but he certainly deserves to be included in pre-Freudian history as he was arguably one of the very first to practice a form of psychotherapy. In 1838, after witnessing a demonstration of mesmerism, Quimby started practising it himself, and initially was a firm believer in animal magnetism. But although he achieved good results, he started to evolve the idea that his patients' disorders were often brought about not by disease, but by their beliefs about their conditions. Talking sympathetically to them, he would help them understand that their suffering was an error of mind. He would propose alternative ways of thinking (what he called "the Truth") and so restore them to health, or at least bring about an improvement of their condition. He was a religious man and related his cures to the methods he perceived to have been used by Jesus. He treated rich and poor alike and never charged for his sessions.

Moving one step closer to Freud, in 1841 James Braid (1795–1860), a Scottish physician, having witnessed a demonstration of mesmerism by the Swiss practitioner, Charles Lafontaine (1803–1892), was convinced that the trance induced in the subject was psychological and had nothing to do with magnetism. Nevertheless, Braid was intrigued by the phenomenon of trances, and carried out some simple experiments on volunteers. He would tell them to gaze at bright objects held in front of their eyes and found he could achieve sleep states by suggestion alone. In order to make a clear distinction from mesmerism, he called his process "hypnotism", after the Greek word *hypnos*, meaning "sleep".

In an acerbic letter to the editor of *The Lancet* in 1845, Braid stated:

> I adopted the term "hypnotism" to prevent my being confounded with those who entertain those extreme notions that a mesmeriser's will has an irresistible power over his subjects ... as well as to get rid of the erroneous theory about a magnetic fluid, or exoteric influence of any description being the cause of the sleep.

He went on:

> Further, I have never been a supporter of the imagination theory. My belief is quite the contrary. I attribute it to the induction of a habit of intense abstraction, or concentration of attention, and maintain that it is most readily induced by causing the patient to fix his thoughts and sight on an object, and suppress his respiration.[3]

As will be seen, the dismissive and scornful tone of this letter is quite typical of the clashes that have featured throughout the development of psychotherapy.

Braid's intervention should finally have put paid to the witchcraft and magic that had dominated the interpretation of induced emotional states, but this didn't stop wild practices and claims for mental healing continuing to proliferate. William Atkinson describes the invention of Elisha Perkins (1741–1799) who conceived the idea of curing disease by means of a pair of tongs, one of brass, the other of steel.[4] These so-called "tractors" were stroked over the affected areas of the body for ten minutes. Almost miraculous cures were achieved by this process and, in Europe, it was reported that one and a half million people were cured by "Perkinsism" (much to the frustration of the medical profession).

But if you think the attributes of Perkinsism seem questionable, how about this:

> During the healing session the practitioner will place his hands lightly on different parts of your body. Some practitioners will follow a predetermined sequence of hand placements, allowing their hands to rest on each body placement for 2 to 5 minutes before moving on to the next. Energy automatically flows where the imbalances are in the body, regardless of where the practitioner's hands are placed.[5]

This is a description of Reiki, a healing technique that supposedly involves using "life force energy" (translation of *Ki*) to achieve its effects. Whatever your instinctive views, this is a method widely and successfully practised in the UK today, so there are no rules as to what counts as legitimate.

But there are three factors that can be derived from these "treatments", all of which will be seen to impact on counselling.

The first of these is that a high level of focused, personal attention can, in itself, be extremely therapeutic for the person receiving it. The second is that the human psyche, when programmed to do so, exerts impressive powers to impact on both the physical and psychological states of the individual. The third is the potentially dangerous human tendency to respond unquestioningly to instructions from someone they believe to be in a position of authority. This last phenomenon has been demonstrated in chilling experiments, of which more later.

The ability of the human mind to be open to suggestion, whilst vital in hypnosis, has been something of a bugbear in both psychiatry and medicine. This is what produces the placebo effect in which an inactive substance, such as a sugar or saline solution can improve a patient's condition simply because the person has the expectation that it will be helpful. There is now a recognized classification called MUS (medically unexplained symptoms) in which patients present with physical manifestations that lack an obvious organic basis and which appear to be psychologically induced. We'll be exploring the implications of this for psychotherapy later in the book.

Meanwhile, back to James Braid. Following his identification of hypnosis, the psychological value of this process rapidly gained respect and authority. The French physician Ambroise-Auguste Liébeault (1823–1904) formed the Nancy school of "suggestive therapeutics" in which Liébeault would propose to patients he had hypnotized that they would recover from a range of disorders they saw themselves as inflicted with, from indigestion to coughing to sleeplessness. In 1889, his colleague, Hippolyte Bernheim (1840–1919), wrote a comprehensive book on the subject, *Suggestive Therapeutics: A Treatise on the Nature and Uses of Hypnotism*, which is still in print to this day.

This was the fertile ground in which Sigmund Freud was able to make his huge contribution to psychotherapy through the development of psychoanalysis. As is so often the case with therapeutic approaches, the development of psychoanalysis was strongly influenced by past endeavours to understand the human psyche and Freud's own characteristics, background, and training.

Freud initially set out to become a doctor in the accepted sense. He joined the medical faculty at the University of Vienna, but found his principal interests lay in the science of physiology and the links between cause and effect in biology. He gravitated towards research, and from 1876 to 1882 worked on the anatomy of the central nervous system in the laboratory of Ernst Brücke (1819–1892), a pioneer in developing an understanding of fundamental life processes. Brücke sought to break down complex organic structures and processes into basic components, the better to understand their interactions. This form of investigation—termed "reductionism"—perfectly suited Freud's analytical mind. Freud stated that Brücke was the highest authority that ever had influence on him.

For his part, Brücke was pleased with Freud's thoroughness and dedication. He arranged for him to go to Paris and study the experimental work of the French neurologist, Jean-Martin Charcot (1825–1893). Charcot was a brilliant physician doing pioneering work in joint disease and the impact of diabetes. As part of his research, Charcot was exploring the use of hypnosis on patients in an attempt to discover the origin of a variety of unexplained physical symptoms including paralysis, seizures, and contractures—a form of muscle spasm that results in the body adopting bizarre postures.

Charcot believed that these symptoms were all manifestations of hysteria, a description for excessive or uncontrollable emotional disturbance. Charcot designated hysteria as a neurological disorder, but speculated that some episodes may have their origins in a particular traumatic event from the past, such as a fall or other accident. Hypnosis could bring out the memory of these events, which had previously been hidden. Freud was intrigued by this idea and began to form the notion that the conscious and the unconscious could be separate entities not always connecting with one another.

Here Freud had a stroke of luck. Just as he was taking his final medical exams a friend of his, Josef Breuer (1842–1925), some ten years his senior, told him about a young woman he was treating, under the pseudonym of Anna O, who was suffering from a range of disturbances following the death of her father. She first developed a cough, then distortions of vision, then headaches, and then episodes of paralysis and loss of balance. At times, she became muddled in her use of language, or would speak only English. Freud thought that these symptoms might not be related to physical causes, but could actually be a reflection of her grieving emotional state. The most significant aspect of this case was that Anna O would alternate between a world of bizarre mental disorder and periods of complete lucidity—a clear indication that her unconscious mind had been intruding on her conscious perceptions. Inevitably, given the prevailing climate, her case was diagnosed as hysteria.

Importantly, Anna O was able to recognize in her lucid periods the impact of her unconscious disturbances and under light hypnosis was able to talk of the issues that had been troubling her. Breuer found that this "talking cure", Anna's own description of the process, relieved her of the associated symptoms—a process she described as "chimney sweeping". As therapy proceeded, Breuer found it wasn't always necessary to hypnotize Anna. Just letting her talk freely was calming in itself. Freud was fascinated by the idea that the way to cure a particular symptom of hysteria was to recreate the memory of the incident that had originally led to it. He was also intrigued that a suggestion could be made to someone under hypnosis and that she might later act on it, having forgotten what it was she had been told to do.

Breuer's treatment of Anna O is sometimes referred to as the first example of psychoanalysis, but although it represented progress towards a psychological approach to therapy, there was much that remained unexplained. Freud realized that the lapses in memory Breuer had recovered from Anna O were a product of part of the mind which ordinary enquiry would not reveal. But just what was being revealed and what was being held back? And not only what, but why?

Freud completed his medical degree and after a spell at Vienna General Hospital went into practice as a specialist in the treatment of psychological disorders. As would be expected, given his training and expectations, all his patients were women and all "hysterics", referred to him because they seemed to display the physical symptoms associated with hysteria. Initially, he dealt with them using hypnosis to uncover the traumatic incident that supposedly gave rise to their symptoms. But he felt the response to hypnosis didn't tell the whole story. There were gaps, and on his own admission, he wasn't very good at hypnotism. Instead, he put his patients into a state of concentration, sometimes applying pressure on their foreheads to facilitate the process. Following on from Breuer's treatment of Anna O, he encouraged his patients to talk about whatever came into their minds—a process called "free association". But he found that at some point the patient's stream of words would often falter. Freud detected resistance—a force separate from the person's will that intervened to stop the flow.

Freud's scientific background, developed through his training under Brücke and Charcot, provided the impetus to explore more deeply the elements that comprise the human mind. He formed the hypothesis that the mind was a dynamic entity of several parts, conscious and unconscious, operating sometimes in harmony and sometimes in opposition to one another. He determined that there were active parts of the mind that were not always available, either to the patient or the therapist.

He developed a compelling metaphor to describe three aspects that comprise the personality: the id, ego, and super-ego. The id (Latin for "it") he defined as the most primitive part of our psyche, the dinosaur concerned only with pleasure and the avoidance of pain. The id is impulsive, and demands immediate gratification. (Far too much id around today, some might think!) The id has no interest in anyone's well-being, only its own.

The ego, or "I", is that part of us which tries to modify the demands of the id by reference to the real world. The ego, too, is concerned with gratifying our desires, but recognizes that a strategy may be needed to achieve this. Freud suggested that if the id is a horse, then the ego is its rider. But to continue the analogy, it could be said that the horse is wilful and the rider too easily led in directions of the horse's choosing. If challenged, the ego is likely to defend the demands of the id on the grounds that its actions were justifiable.

The final component, the super-ego, represents the moral part of the personality and consists of two parts: the conscience and the ideal self. It is the super-ego that is our inner voice, the one that tells us how we ought to be. On the one hand, it is the reward we feel when we have behaved in accordance with our moral codes, but equally it is the voice of reproach when we haven't performed as well as we know we should, and which is responsible for emotions like guilt and shame. Both ego and super-ego are very much the product of our upbringing and the society in which we live.

A simple example illustrates the concept. A small child, on seeing that another child has a bag of sweets, might well crawl over and help himself to some. This is the id, pure and simple. As he gets older, the child knows he must first ask—not out of any moral drive, but because he'll be in trouble if he doesn't. This is the ego seeking a way of satisfying the id. If he is refused, he might wait until the other child isn't looking and then steal a sweet. If he does this and is caught, he will likely be very defensive because he knows he has misbehaved.

But even if he gets away with it, he may feel ashamed or guilty. This is the super-ego stepping in, reminding him that if everyone carried on with disregard for other people's possessions, life would be impossible.

In counselling, the interaction of id, ego, and super-ego can sometimes create quite misleading presentations.

Consider the case of Alison. She comes for counselling ostensibly because she is worried about her marriage. She says she suspects her husband may be having an affair, although she has no direct evidence to this effect. They have rows and arguments and she claims that he says unkind things to her. If he brings her presents or is considerate, it can only be because he has a guilty conscience.

This presentation may seem straightforward enough, but the reality is rather different. What has actually happened is that Alison has fallen for someone else. Her id wants her to have a passionate affair with this other man. But she knows that if she just walks out on her husband, she'll attract a good deal of opprobrium which could damage her reputation. Therefore, she needs the role of the wronged wife, and her ego has been set the task of achieving this. Her hope is that the counsellor will advise her to leave him (but counsellors do not give advice or tell their clients what to do).

The real dichotomy here is that her super-ego reminds her that her husband is a good man who has always cared for her and if she had any decency she would stay with him. She also subconsciously recalls that the father of a friend of hers had an affair and she was deeply critical of this man's actions for threatening his family's life. What does it say about her if she behaves no better? She feels guilty and ashamed at the thought, but resents the fact. So the real dichotomy is between ego and super-ego.

The repression of the unconscious sometimes manifests itself in so-called "Freudian slips", in which a mistake in speech reveals something of the nature of the speaker's unconscious or semi-conscious desires. A classic example was when, then prime minister, Gordon Brown, slipped up in a debate in the Commons in which he intended to claim he had saved the banks but said instead that he had saved the world, thus perhaps revealing a wish for universal empowerment.

* * *

As mentioned earlier, Freud's patients were invariably young women who had been diagnosed as "hysterics".

The concept of "hysteria" had existed since Roman times and was deemed to be brought about by displacement of the uterus through lack of sexual activity. From this, Freud drew the conclusion that all psychopathology was sexual. This may seem overly simplistic but it is worth considering for a moment the social environment in which he practised. If you decide to pursue a career in counselling you'll find that external factors play a huge part in how you work. Social attitudes and perceptions, interpretations of mental health, and the impact of political doctrine, will all profoundly influence how you practice and how your clients respond.

In the Victorian era social correctness in relation to women was a powerful force. Cole Porter's lyric "In olden days a glimpse of stocking was look'd on as something shocking" (from the musical *Anything Goes*) is no exaggeration. Prudery ruled, with some bizarre consequences. This was a time when a woman was expected to keep her body covered, even when taking a bath in her own home. The hems of Victorian skirts touched the floor because to allow an ankle to be seen was regarded as irresponsibly provocative. There was a form of Political Correctness in place even then; the use of the word "leg" in circumstances where it might conjure up unsuitable images was replaced by the more refined term "limb". It is even said that Victorians pulled stockings over the legs of their pianos for fear of their seeming erotic, although this is probably fictional. In any event, the concept of women having sexual feelings was inconceivable. Queen Victoria even passed a law stating that women could never be accused of self-induced orgasm.

This prudery contrasted sharply with a lively market in Victorian erotica. Mistresses (known as one's "convenient") were commonplace. There was an inventive vocabulary of sexual slang to cover every conceivable event and to provide a lingo for those seeking conjugal activity outside the home.

In this environment, it was hardly surprising that unmarried women or those with inattentive husbands experienced huge sexual frustration which often emerged in their dreams. Freud realized that dreams could be a gateway for revealing memories while the psyche was "off-line", and in his book *The Interpretation of Dreams* (1899) described them as "The Royal Road to the Unconscious". He further declared that every dream was an attempt to fulfil a wish dating from early childhood. He construed these wishes as invariably having a sexual context and from this developed the Oedipus complex, which assumes that the son unconsciously sees in his father a rival to sexual fulfilment and fears that he will attempt to castrate him. (The Electra complex reflected the daughter's unconscious sexual attraction towards her father.)

Whilst sexual abuse can certainly be the cause of trauma, the assumption that in some form it is behind all hidden memories perhaps rather illustrates the maxim devised by another analyst, Abraham Maslow (1908–1970), which is that "to the man with a hammer every problem is a nail". We develop our theories of how negative emotions or unproductive behaviour come about from our own experiences, and it is tempting, in the role of counsellor, to assume that our clients will be doing the same. Equally, if a person has been trained in one particular therapeutic approach it may be instinctive to adopt the same approach with everyone. Clients, too, will be deeply influenced by the environment in which they live, so the capacity for open-mindedness and the avoidance of dogma in the counsellor are essential to productive therapy. This is a theme we will return to in later chapters.

Freud's view of the significance of the libido was such that he believed that he could do less for older patients whose sexual drive would be much reduced. But although he still attached enormous importance to the influence of sex in psychoanalysis, he came to the conclusion that sexual elements were not the whole story. He recognized, too, that an approach in which the therapist used his authority to guide the patient through suggestion limited the information he would obtain. It was this that led him to adopt the idea of free association in which he would invite patients to talk about whatever came into their mind. Often he would say very little. His technique was to let his patients find their own way forward.

What Freud established with free association is that all human behaviour and thought processes are open to exploration and, once analysed, become understandable. The very fact of a patient realizing how she had been emotionally handicapped, often by events taking place in childhood, could be enlightening and curative. Freud continued to develop and refine this approach throughout his life as an analyst. Those following him made their own contributions, not always in accord with Freud, but emanating from his ideas.

A note at this point: Individuals coming for counselling today are termed "clients", reflecting the fact that they have engaged the services of a therapist on their own initiative. But in Freud's day they were "patients", referred to him as requiring medical treatment, much as would someone who had a physical disorder.

Freud had his critics, and those following on focused on different aspects of his work, but he deservedly occupies a prime place in creating an understanding of the workings of the human mind.

* * *

Some factors from all of the above are worth considering at this point, since they are likely to impact on therapists' approach to their work.

We have a natural tendency to be selective in our thinking according to our life experiences and to adopt hypotheses for living and working which accord with these experiences. In doing so, we may unwittingly ignore factors that run counter to our conceptions. Perhaps because of his own background, Freud was determined that psychoanalysis should be given the status of a science—a view frequently disputed by later practitioners. He therefore avoided elements of the consultation that were unpredictable or which interfered with the analysis he was conducting. The life experiences of therapists who followed him similarly served as a focus for the success of their approaches, but also their limitations.

Freud noticed that some of his patients started to develop strong feelings for and fantasies about him that had no basis in reality, a phenomenon that we know as "transference". An extreme example of this emerged when he later started working with Breuer. Far from being cured of her symptoms, it transpired that Anna O had started inventing psychoses to continue her association with Breuer. Matters reached a head when she announced she was pregnant with Breuer's baby and apparently began experiencing morning sickness! Breuer, a married man, became alarmed, and called a stop to treating her. (The story ends better than might be expected; Anna O recovered over time and led a productive life as a social worker.)

Freud regarded transference as a curse, as it corrupted the science of psychoanalysis and was embarrassing to boot. He would have his patients lie on a couch and would sit behind them to minimize contact and keep the transactions as impersonal as possible. He was aware that transference was a two-way street and that he could be emotionally affected by his patients, a process known as "countertransference". Freud discovered, as had Breuer before him, that some sexual experiences were actually sexual fantasies and that patients would compromise their presenting symptoms if they chose to.

This is an important consideration for the counsellor. We are only able to work with what our clients give us, whatever our preferred theories or expectations. The neutrality of the therapist is important in this regard, as there is no benefit, however convenient it may seem at the time, in putting ideas into clients' minds. But whilst transference and countertransference can impact significantly on counselling, they can also be seen as useful for the information about the client they can reveal. We will be exploring this further in the following chapter.

Another major contribution to psychotherapy was Freud's recognition of the importance of the therapist thoroughly understanding himself. He realized that his own prejudices could corrupt the impartiality that was vital to the therapeutic process. In the absence of anyone else, he did psychoanalysis on himself, reflecting deeply on the impact of his childhood and his relationship with his father. He was not without his own neuroses. Even whilst formulating his ideas, he experienced massive anxiety about death and long journeys. But he utilized his self-knowledge to furnish him with insight into his patients' neurotic states. His willingness to give balanced consideration to all the information at his disposal enabled him to modify his approach as needed.

It is unlikely you would be practising true psychoanalysis, not least because of the cost, as it is based on clients having three or more sessions a week. Psychoanalysis has been largely replaced by psychodynamic therapy, which has a significant following in the UK. It says much for Freud's writings that the great majority of the books in which he wrote about all aspects of his work are still in print. If you are interested in learning more, *Freud: A Very Short Introduction* (2001) by Anthony Storr, is an accessible study of his life and work, and, for more detail, *The Freud Reader* (1995) is an edited collection of his writings, well translated, and which also shows the human side of him.

The next major event in the development of psychology occurred in 1906 when Freud received a volume of studies from a Dr Carl Jung, senior psychiatrist at the Burghlözli mental hospital in Zürich. Jung had been conducting experiments in word association with his patients. He recognized the impact of the unconscious on his results and readily acknowledged in his book the importance of Freud's work in psychoanalysis. Freud was delighted. He was now aged fifty. Other doctors were imitating his methods but he was concerned that many only imperfectly understood the process. He was acutely conscious that there was no one whom he could regard as a successor. He arranged to meet Jung and the stage was set for the next chapter in the development of psychological understanding and therapeutic practice.

Notes

1. Atkinson, W. W. (1910). Mind and body or mental states and physical conditions. Chapter Five: *The History of Psycho-Therapy* (p. 84). Hollister, MO: YOGeBooks.
2. (2009, October 3). Pick of the week's gossip. *The Week.*
3. Braid, J. (1845). Mr Braid on hypnotism. *The Lancet, 45 (1135)*: 627–628. (Reproduced with permission.)
4. About.com. What is Reiki? *Holistic Healing*.
5. Atkinson, W. W. (1910). Mind and body or mental states and physical conditions. Chapter Five: *The History of Psycho-Therapy* (p. 99). Hollister, MO: YOGeBooks.

CHAPTER TWO

The age of psychoanalysis

When Freud and Jung first met, a huge rapport immediately developed. The story goes that they talked virtually without a break for thirteen hours! Jung saw Freud as a father figure, his own father having died when he was young. Freud regarded Jung, twenty years his junior, as his heir-apparent. But a friendship that started so promisingly and blossomed for some seven years, nevertheless ended in acrimony, accusations, counter-accusations, and mutual dislike. Was the breakdown inevitable? Although it may not provide all the answers, one of the essential elements of counselling is recognizing the impact of significant events in childhood, our own every bit as much as those of our clients. Social background, relationships with parents, siblings, and other family members, and the established criteria for what constituted good or bad behaviour, success or failure, all play their part. As Aristotle said: "If you would understand anything, observe its beginning and its development."

From the outset, Freud's and Jung's backgrounds were very different. Freud was the eldest of five children from his father's second marriage, and his mother's favourite. She encouraged him to be ambitious and always believed he would be a success. Freud was proudly Jewish in an anti-Semitic culture and determined to prove himself. Money was tight, but his parents scraped together enough to send him to medical school. Freud thus started his adult life imbued with confidence and the determination to merit his parents' investment in him and, through success, to avoid the strictures of poverty.

Jung, on the other hand, was an only child growing up in a deeply religious environment. His father was a clergyman, as were many of his uncles. His mother was an eccentric whose behaviour was normal during the day, but who became strange and capricious at night. Jung was fearful of her unpredictability and would experience weird dreams in which ghosts and spirits played a major part. Perhaps following on from his mother, he began to think of himself as having two personalities: the first, a natural one of everyday life, and a second that was foggy and unfathomable. He had great difficulty in reconciling these.

His inability to separate the two sides of himself made it hard for Jung to decide on what he wanted to do. Part of him was attracted to science with its truths based on facts, but his other side remained troublesomely dissatisfied. In the meantime, he had to earn a living. He recalled that his grandfather had been a doctor and saw in this a certain freedom, in that he had a choice to practice that part of medicine that interested him. He became a junior assistant in anatomy, but, unlike Freud, was uncomfortable with the animal dissection that was a feature of experimental physiology.

Then, in his second year, Jung came across a book on the birth of spiritualism and realized that the ancient tales it told were remarkably similar to the stories he had heard in his own childhood. This led him to believe that there must be a deeper layer of the unconscious, inherited from man's ancestral past; a past that included not only the history of humankind but its pre-human or animal existence as well. He later found that American Indians and Africans shared similar stories. These peoples had no contact with one another, yet their legends were the same. From this he drew the idea of a "collective unconscious" derived from a shared humanity, and began to study mythology with its symbols, dreams, and visions.

As a part of his student training he had to read about psychiatry, but didn't find prevailing attitudes to mental health very inspiring. This was at a time when mental disorders were not well understood and psychiatry considered a fairly hopeless occupation. Then he came across a book in which the author described psychotic states as "diseases of the personality". "That," said Jung in an interview many years later, "hit the nail on the head and I knew psychiatry was my destiny." His tutors were dismayed at his choice, but Jung saw this as a chance to reconcile science with philosophy.

Jung was apprenticed to the famous Burghölzli, psychiatric hospital of the University of Zürich, Switzerland. Here was a place where reality had little meaning and no assumptions could be made based on the usual criteria of cause and effect. As such, it was the perfect environment for him to explore what went on in the minds of the mentally affected. But he was disappointed to find that work at the hospital focused less on the personalities of the patients and what might be going on in their minds than on compiling statistics and rubber-stamping diagnoses. This may seem largely to miss the point of mental healthcare but, in many ways, approaches to mental health are not dissimilar today. All too often, patients experiencing psychological problems, both in mental institutions and outside, are labelled and medicated according to standardized diagnostic criteria, a situation that inspired a young mental health worker, Ken Kesey, to write his seminal novel *One Flew Over the Cuckoo's Nest* (1962).

Cautiously, since he was only a junior, Jung started carrying out his own investigations. He talked to patients, with sometimes bizarre results. Jung put into a trance one woman who had been lame for several years and when he wakened her she leapt to her feet and announced herself cured—much to his embarrassment as he had no idea how this had happened. He steered clear of hypnosis after that.

But other contacts showed him that patients had stories, some of which were revealed by their dreams, which seemed to reflect his view of the shared experiences of humanity. Jung began to see the importance of assessing the patient as a whole rather than as the product of a set of symptoms. Having few kindred spirits with whom he could exchange ideas, Freud's work on psychology and dreams assumed enormous importance for him. It was in 1906, by which time he was senior physician at the Burghölzli, that he sent Freud his book of studies on word association.

So Freud and Jung arrived at psychiatry by very different routes. Freud sought to create a scientific model of the mind which would stand scrutiny and the components of which, particularly resistance, could be readily identified. For him, the goal of therapy was to relieve his patients' symptoms by helping them recall forgotten memories and overcome unconscious resistance.

Jung's theory of a personal unconscious was quite similar to Freud's, in that it contained a person's repressed, forgotten, or ignored experiences, but his background led him to believe that there were spiritual and hereditary elements in the unconscious that may be unknown to the individual. So whilst Freud preferred to let the patient discover their unconscious thinking, Jung thought this was too difficult for them. He believed his patients needed help to understand themselves, that his interpretation was essential, and that we cannot make progress unless we are able to distinguish between our instinctual self-knowledge and that which is imposed upon us from outside. Whilst Freud was primarily concerned with his patients' past, Jung was more interested in what their future might hold as a consequence of his talks with them. He called his approach "analytical psychology" to distinguish it from psychoanalysis.

Were there aspects Freud and Jung agreed upon? Jung used many of the same terms as Freud, such as "ego" and "unconscious", but they held a different meaning when considered in the light of Jung's whole theory. Somewhat akin to Freud's id is The Shadow— that part of ourselves we do not like: dangerous, primitive, and unscrupulous. The Shadow is derived from our pre-human past: an entity without emotion, being concerned only with its own survival.

Then there is The Persona, which reflects the way we seek to be identified in society. In its simplest interpretation The Persona is a mask we adopt to give people some idea of what we do or to furnish them with reassurance. Thus, the director of an art gallery may opt for a slightly flamboyant style of dress and sport a goatee beard. This would fit in with our expectations. A bank manager is likely to wear a dark suit and a tie. His clients might well be less confident if he appeared for a meeting wearing a Hawaiian shirt and a baseball cap back to front, although it would make no difference to his skills.

The man who spends a four figure sum acquiring a personalized number plate for his car may be hoping that we will accord him some status of importance or simply that we'll notice him. We also have different personas according to circumstances. Thus, the most gentle and tender of mothers at home may have a justified reputation as a tough and uncompromising manager at work.

The Persona offers an excellent source for acquiring self-knowledge, as it reflects the relationship between who we are and how we present to the world. When we find ourselves in a social or work setting in which we feel obscurely uncomfortable, or start to conduct ourselves in a way that seems at odds with our usual behaviour, it can be instructive to explore the reasons why we are feeling as we are. The realization, for example, that someone we're talking to subconsciously reminds us of an authoritarian schoolteacher from our childhood enables us to decide on how we manage ourselves in their presence as an adult.

Freud and Jung also shared the idea that everyone has some element of the male and female in them. Jung called the man within the woman "the animus", and the woman within the man, "the anima". Jung also detected in people a range of archetypes—patterns of thought and behaviour inherited from our past shared experience. So the hero, the villain, the father, and the family share characteristics recognized in heroes, villains, fathers, and families everywhere. These archetypes recur in fairy stories, legends, and fables as evidence of our collective unconscious.

Jung took the view that rather than sticking to one set procedure with specific guidelines, the therapist should adapt his approach to the individual's needs and avoid theoretical assumptions. This did not mean abandoning the proper boundaries and normal disciplines, but, a major difference from Freud, Jung regarded the relationship between doctor and patient as one of partners working together. He conducted his analysis facing his patients, thereby conferring authority on them to take part. This enabled him to benefit from the additional information they gave him in their facial expressions and body language. As he was not looking for resistance as the key to finding a resolution, he avoided confrontation and focused his attention on helping his patients to better understand themselves. In another major step forward, he moved away from the idea that the patient had to have a neurosis to be a candidate for treatment, recognizing that "normal" people experience difficulties that the therapist can address.

So even at this early stage, Jung was starting to bring to counselling many of the features that are practised today.

Freud had published a book in 1899, *The Interpretation of Dreams*, but was disappointed by the reception it received. He wrote to a colleague in 1900: "Not a leaf has stirred to reveal that *The Interpretation of Dreams* has had any impact on anyone." Jung, however, shared his view that dream interpretation was a valuable resource in researching the unconscious. Freud thought of dreams as a symbolic representation of repressed desires and that their purpose was to compensate for the way in which the conscious could not express itself. This could well match his experience in dealing with hysterics. So he distinguished between the manifest content of the dream, which the patient would easily recall, and the latent part, which the patient subconsciously withheld. He considered that this may reflect the conflict between ego and super-ego.

Although not dismissing Freud's model of dream analysis wholesale, Jung believed his notion that they solely represented unfulfilled wishes to be simplistic. He agreed there were elements that were symbolic, but felt it was dangerous to take a dogmatic approach to their interpretation. He regarded dreams as metaphors that should be explored for their personal significance to the individual.

How much do dreams feature in counselling today? It is unlikely that a client will come to counselling solely to talk about dreams, but once therapy is underway the subject does crop up quite often.

Take the case of Henry (not his real name), a successful salesman travelling often to Europe and the States. He revealed that on one trip he had planned to visit an established customer but, on impulse, decided instead to call on a potentially major new prospect. Being unfamiliar with the journey to the company's office he arrived late, to find that the people to whom he had hoped to make his presentation had gone off to other meetings. He realized that this probably cost him dear and resolved not to repeat the mistake. He felt guilty that he had made the wrong choice: he should have seen his other clients. Not long after this, he found that he had a recurring nightmare in which he breathlessly turned up for meetings at which no one was present. These meetings could take place anywhere: in an old barn, a small room, a vast hall, or an open space. He would awake in a high state of anxiety, which he resented, feeling that he had learned his lesson at the time and shouldn't have to have his knuckles repeatedly rapped for an error.

His background revealed that there were circumstances that may have contributed to this ongoing anxiety. His mother had died when he was twelve, and when he was twenty-one his elder sister, to whom he was very close, was killed in a road accident. These two tragic events impacted on him very severely. When he was in his twenties, he met a girl, Lisa, and it seemed likely at first that they would stay together. But while they had much in common, their temperaments didn't quite match. A history developed of their breaking up and getting back together again for another trial run, usually at Henry's instigation. He met other women but found he couldn't go forward with a new relationship without his one with Lisa being resolved. Although forthright and outwardly confident—talents necessary for his salesmanship—he recognized that when confronted with a simple choice he would often have great difficulty making up his mind. He cited as examples choosing between two shirts or two ties for work or two different plants for his garden. Whatever he finally chose, he would agonize as to whether he had made the right decision. He would often end up buying both items he was struggling over, or neither.

It is likely that the bereavements he had experienced at a critical age had made it very difficult for him to deal with loss. What if he did finally let his relationship with Lisa go? What if he did select one shirt over another? What he did not choose he would, by definition, lose. The sales meeting episode which haunted his dreams represented a double blow; not only did he forfeit the opportunity to call on his old client, he lost seeing a potential new one, too.

With a better understanding of the significance of these life events, Henry felt able to assume more authority over himself. His nightmares became flimsier and eventually dissipated. He remained friends with Lisa but felt freer to pursue his own interests. These were not the only issues that were dealt with in sessions and it could well be argued that the dream could be analysed in a totally different way. But progress in counselling can legitimately be represented as a process of self-discovery which enables the client to achieve a better understanding of him or herself.

The idea of being able to access aspects of a person's mind that are unconsciously troubling them is an appealing one, potentially offering dividends in any therapeutic setting. You don't have to have psychic powers or have completed a counselling course to interpret dreams, and as an exercise it can be quite revealing, not only for potential future clients but also for oneself. Like most skills, it requires practice and a logical approach, themselves good disciplines.

If we are questioned about what we might have dreamed the following morning we may well remember the main theme but will probably be unable to recall aspects of the dream which could be valuable. The only way to be sure of capturing as much as possible (except for the bit you might, Freudian-style, unconsciously be concealing) is to describe your dream in detail as soon as you awake. You can write your thoughts down, but if you are still a little bleary-eyed it may be easier to record them on disc or tape. For that you'll need a recorder. We're not looking for high-definition here, so anything will do, but preferably a machine with a pause button. Every aspect in a dream needs noting: the location, the people around you, what they say, what you say, as well as the general theme, and how consistent the story. Note how you felt: happy, frightened, bewildered, sad, or guilty. Record also the environment: day, night, sunny, cold. Make a record of your clothes, other people's ... See if you had acquired new skills in the dream such as flying or scaling walls to give yourself the freedom to be where you wanted to go.

You will then need to transcribe your recordings so that you can scan the content. Look for links between dreams, within them, and for situations that may not make immediate sense. Try to see if there could be some meaning that is not immediately obvious. Following the Jungian approach, you might look for symbols or metaphors which could direct you to past experiences. Freudians would be looking for wish-fulfilment or resistance. Such elements will more likely be in the detail rather than the main content, but both are valid concepts. You are uniquely privileged as being the only person to have experienced every aspect of your own life history and are therefore, theoretically, perfectly positioned to use the material to good effect.

That said, it is important not to demand that you identify some hugely meaningful element in every dream, or that you too rigidly categorize the content. The Internet has a plethora of websites claiming to be able to analyse every aspect of dreams to standard criteria but these should be approached with caution. Bear in mind that not every dream, or aspect of a dream, is going to be significant. Part of the purpose of dreaming is to process new data while the system is "off-line", rather as a computer has to close down after filing updates in order for them to be properly incorporated.

So, with your self-knowledge in place, if a friend buttonholes you and says, "I had the weirdest dream last night ... ", you might be able to use the information, with judicious questioning, to good effect!

* * *

As mentioned in the previous chapter, a phenomenon which Freud distrusted, but which frequently occurs in the counselling environment, is transference. "Transference" describes the displacement of feelings from one person to another. We can probably all recall occasions when we have met someone and instinctively liked or disliked him, even before we have got to know him. What is often happening here is that we are transferring onto this individual emotions that developed in another relationship because some aspect of him takes us back to it.

If we were made to believe that we were inadequate in some way by a parent or teacher, we may well unconsciously expect that every new person we meet of a certain appearance or manner will feel the same way about us. In these situations, we may develop strategies to try to hide these instinctive feelings, perhaps with a show of extrovert behaviour or by professing disinterest in the other person's views. Therapists provide stability, so it is not surprising that in an intimate, prolonged relationship some clients develop romantic feelings towards their counsellors. This can be particularly so where the therapist may be seen to represent someone in their lives whom they feel should love or appreciate them, but who perhaps does not.

Clients who idealize their therapists may be profusely complimentary, do all they can to please them, and may even adopt their style of speech or wear similar clothing. They may be inclined to endow the therapist with unrealistic potential, assuming she will know the answers to all their questions. But if they feel the counsellor fails to meet their expectations in any way, they may become angry or uncooperative.

On the other hand, the client who looks to the therapist to assume the role of carer may present as helpless and overtly dependent on her for advice and guidance at every level. They may seek physical contact, holding hands or being cuddled, but as a child to a parent rather than as a potential sexual partner. These unconscious characteristics may emerge unexpectedly, but they all provide material to reveal unresolved conflicts.

Countertransference occurs when difficulties therapists themselves may have are activated by the client. If the counsellor feels the need to be liked or to be considered important, she may well unwittingly encourage dependence on the part of the client or offer advice for the sake of seeming all-knowing.

Think about how you might respond if you were a counsellor and a client was always late, appeared to be sulking during sessions, seemed disdainful of your professional skills, or consistently denied that any progress was being made. What if you discovered that the client had characteristics that you personally found abhorrent, would you succeed in maintaining an impartial approach? If you realized you were alternating between empathy with your client and experiencing profound irritation and impatience with them, then you would clearly need to know what was going on. The therapist's awareness of their own countertransference, therefore, is at least as critical as understanding the process of transference.

This is not to suggest that the counsellor must suffer in silence and it may be in the interests of the therapeutic relationship for them to give some feedback to the client by explaining their feelings, although this is always a matter of careful judgement.

Another aspect of transference might almost be called "counter-countertransference". This is when the client has become aware of the counsellor's countertransference and transfers their recognition of this back to them, possibly seeking to take advantage of their knowledge to manipulate the session. These factors, if not successfully managed, clearly have the potential for impacting negatively on the relationship.

All these caveats may seem rather alarming, but most transference and countertransference situations can be managed once they are recognized.

It is worth noting at this point that therapists don't work in isolation. It is a requirement for all counsellors to have a supervisor. This is a rather misleading term. It does not mean someone standing over them to make sure they get it right, but rather an experienced person with whom they can discuss issues arising from their sessions and who will offer support and guidance in dealing with more intractable matters that may be arising.

* * *

As mentioned at the beginning of the chapter, the bond between Freud and Jung eventually broke down. This arose partly because Jung was not comfortable with the role Freud ascribed to him as his heir and successor, which clearly depended on his following, as a faithful disciple, every aspect of his theories. Jung felt unable to do this, not least because he could not agree with Freud's dogma that sexual drives were at the root of all neuroses. For his part, Freud dismissed Jung's concept of the "collective unconscious" and disliked what he called "occultism", stating that it impacted negatively on the scientific structure of psychoanalysis. But as Jung later stated in a television interview: "Where Freud was certain, I had doubts."

A further significant rift occurred when Freud and Jung were on their way to a lecture tour in the United States. To while away the time on the boat, Jung suggested that they analyse one another's dreams. Freud refused to cooperate, however, declaring that to do so would undermine his authority. But, as Jung later observed: "At that moment he lost his authority."

A complete split finally came when Jung published a book in which he opposed Freud's view that the libido was a purely sexual expression, maintaining that it represented psychic energy. This was *lèse-majesté* of a high order and the friendship was abruptly terminated. Unfortunately, for Jung, his book was not well received and he went through a period of depression. But, like Freud, he spent much time in self-analysis and refining his techniques. Here his face-to-face approach, and his open-mindedness concerning his patients' stories, served him well. He continued to pursue his belief that people cannot change what they do not understand and to clarify the interaction between intuition, sensation, thinking and feeling, and how these related to the type of person they were.

Some psychoanalysts of the period regarded the split between Freud and Jung as a disaster, but I don't believe it should be looked at in this way. Both made a huge contribution to our knowledge of the complexities of the human mind. Also, other notable psychoanalysts who started as orthodox Freudians diverged from his philosophy as they brought their own ideas into the field. As a link to the next chapter, let's consider briefly the contributions of two other significant practitioners of the period.

The first of these, Alfred Adler (1870–1937), was also a colleague of Freud but he too fell out with him, opposing his views that sexual trauma was invariably the cause of mental difficulties. Like Jung, he discarded the couch in favour of face-to-face consultations. Adler was a skilled interpreter but did not want to waste time getting results and would pre-empt his patients' conclusions with his own ideas. The patient in his view was not so much the victim of circumstances, but someone who had made bad choices in life. He moved away from the idea of all problems being derived from the unconscious, insisting that his patients knew what was wrong with them; it was his job to help them adopt more productive thinking so they could take their proper place in society. This active-directive approach required that patients acknowledge their goals and recognize how dysfunctional thinking may have inhibited their progress. Adler sought to see the individual as an integrated being, the product of all aspects of themselves, rather than simply the parts that seemed not to be working.

He believed that the overriding motivation in most people is a striving for self-realization, which may be unwittingly frustrated by feelings of inferiority or inadequacy, often stemming from childhood. Based on his own experience, he held that younger siblings endeavour to surpass their older brothers or sisters by acquiring superior skills. (Adler himself was the second of six children. He couldn't walk until he was four because of rickets and cordially loathed his elder brother. But this evoked in him a determination to succeed—a good example of childhood experiences shaping the adult view on life.)

The oldest child, in turn, may find their self-esteem eroded when a new arrival comes on the scene and will adopt techniques to restore it. However, it is the middle child who often feels him or herself being stuck. Hugh Walpole's superbly insightful novel, *Jeremy*, published in 1919, perfectly illustrates the agony and helplessness of being between an older brother and a younger sister. The individual who can't achieve his or her desired status may withdraw from competition and take refuge in mental or physical illness. Women, Adler believed, were particularly subject to feelings of inferiority, and would often fight to attain status in an unequal relationship.

The Adlerian psychotherapist directs the patient's attention to the neurotic attempts they may be making to cope with feelings of inferiority. Once the patient has become aware of these, the therapist builds up their self-esteem, helps them to adopt more realistic goals, and encourages more useful behaviour as well as a stronger social interest. Adler called his technique "individual psychology" to distinguish it from Freud's psychoanalysis and Jung's analytical psychology. In fact, as with Jung's, many aspects of his approach have been adopted by and absorbed into other counselling orientations, particularly the cognitive behavioural therapies, of which more in a later chapter.

A second major influence was Sándor Ferenczi (1873–1933), a close colleague of Freud. Like Adler, Ferenczi set out to improve the efficiency of psychoanalysis by interacting more directly with the patient, a process he called "active therapy". He also introduced discipline into the procedure. He would define a period of treatment at the outset and agree with the patient to end the sessions when no further changes could be expected. Rather than waiting for his patients' thoughts to develop spontaneously, he would encourage a debate as to what might be going on. He, too, rejected the concept of the detached authoritarian observer, and believed that the analyst must have an open attitude of genuine caring in order to help the patient move forward. Ferenczi disagreed with Freud that memories of childhood abuse lay in the imagination. Instead, he took them seriously as accounts of real traumatic events.

One other pioneer deserves a mention: a British neurologist, Alfred Ernest Jones (1879–1958). He was a contemporary of Freud's and his official biographer. All the pioneers of psychotherapy to date have been Swiss, Austrian, or German (excepting Ferenczi, who was Hungarian). It was Jones who brought psychoanalysis to England, although only after a long struggle. The Edwardian medical establishment was highly suspicious of Freudian theory, and it wasn't until 1919 that Jones obtained sufficient support to found the British Psychoanalytical Society (BPS), of which he held the post of president for the next twenty-five years. Even then, it wasn't until 1929 that he persuaded the British Medical Association (BMA) to give psychoanalysis full recognition. The story ahead will show that many other, now well-respected, counselling approaches endured a rough passage, requiring persistence and determination from their originators to be recognized.

Both Ferenczi and Jones were to be influential in the next stage of psychoanalytical development, as will be seen in the following chapter.

* * *

Meanwhile, some points for consideration from the story so far:

The first of these is that there is no right or wrong way of undertaking psychotherapy. Freud's approach to psychoanalysis is not compromised by other practitioners' methodology. Freud, having initiated psychoanalysis, was protective of its integrity, and retained his determination to have it regarded as a science. This limited his ability or willingness to be open to some of the developments that arose from his work. Unfortunately, he tended to sever relationships with those whose views differed from his, sometimes quite acrimoniously, rather than agreeing to disagree.

It is important for counsellors to be flexible in their thinking, whatever their orientation and training. A willingness to learn about other models and draw freely on their techniques enables counsellors to refine their skills and find the most effective way of addressing issues that a client may raise.

One of the intriguing aspects of this branch of healthcare is that every counsellor brings to it a unique life history, set of personal characteristics, and skills in perception, understanding, and interpretation. So no two counsellors are alike. (The same, of course, applies to their clients.)

Psychoanalysis still has its practitioners, some of whom may follow the ordered Freudian style, whilst others may prefer the more spiritual approach favoured by Jung. As mentioned earlier, true psychoanalysis involves three or four sessions a week over a period that may run into years, incurring a significant commitment of time and money from the client, and thus it tends to be practised less than other techniques that are based on weekly meetings.

However, it is important not to think of these pioneering modalities as being quaint or outmoded, rather like a 1950s' Cadillac, all chrome and fins, beautiful in its way, but essentially passé. Both Freud and Jung wrote extensively on all aspects of psychoanalysis and their many books are still in print, which is testimony to their continuing relevance. The modern counterpart, psychodynamic therapy, is one of the most commonly practised in this country. As with psychoanalysis, it focuses on revealing feelings held in the unconscious mind, often originating in childhood, and which may be too painful to be acknowledged. Psychodynamic counselling is designed to help the client develop a greater understanding of themselves as a prelude to recognizing and dealing with their difficulties. As client and counsellor meet usually once weekly, the focus is likely to be more on specific issues.

An important initial stage in counselling, and particularly with psychodynamic therapy, is the assessment. The counsellor, or, in an agency, whoever compiles the intake notes, might initially record the client's presenting problem, the one that is creating the greatest difficulty, as, for example, wanting to be able to say "no" when people make demands, or to be less touchy, or simply to be able to get on with life. But this is only the beginning. The psychodynamic counsellor may well devote the first three or four sessions entirely to assessment—developing their understanding of who the client is before working on the presenting problem. For their part, clients who have agreed to having psychodynamic therapy are likely to be interested not just in how they might recover from the difficulties they are experiencing, but how they got to where they are in the first place.

Determining what is happening in the unconscious mind is not a rapid process, but if you are interested in exploring the detailed complexities of human relationships and helping clients to recognize how past events have been influencing their lives and possibly obstructing progress, psychodynamic therapy can be a rewarding way of working.

However interesting reading about a particular approach to therapy may be, an extra dimension can be added if one can actually see the originator talking about their life and work. There are only one or two very brief sound clips of Freud, but an excellent BBC half-hour documentary made in the 1960s, has Jung, aged eighty-four, talking to the host, John Freeman. Freeman was an extremely proficient interviewer, skilled at coaxing information from his subjects. Jung is a little reticent about certain aspects of his relationship with Freud but is still feisty and talks intriguingly about how he works. The broadcast can be seen on YouTube under *Face to Face with Carl Jung*.

Although detailed stages of childhood sexual and psychological development had been set out by Freud and others, no work was being done directly with children. Freud thought that they were too young to be analysed. However, Ferenczi, who was inclined to believe what his patients said about childhood events as being factual, rather than imagined, felt instinctively that in the right hands useful work could be done. He had observed that a patient of his, a young Viennese woman named Melanie Klein (1882–1960), seemed to have a talent for understanding children. Relationships between patient and therapist being less formal in those days, he took her on as his assistant and encouraged her to develop her observational skills further by working first with her own, and then with other people's children.

Which is what she did, so opening the door to a new phase of psychological discovery.

CHAPTER THREE

The impact of childhood

Childhood events can have a major influence on our lives. In some measure, all of us have unconscious drives and phobias, often originating in our earliest years and which constitute our inner world.

In many ways, Melanie Klein's background provided her with valuable insight into the stresses of childhood. Born in 1882 in Vienna and living until 1960, she was the youngest of four children and felt unwanted from the outset. Her mother had breastfed her brother and two older sisters but handed Melanie over to a wet nurse. Her father, a surgeon, preferred her sister Emilie. Melanie recalled with some bitterness the time when she tried to climb onto his knee and he pushed her off, leaving her a victim of jealousy, helplessness, and envy. She set out to study medicine and psychiatry, initially in the hope of pleasing her father. But then he died, and she married a man introduced to her by her brother, whose intellect she had always respected. She realized she had made a mistake almost from the outset, but persevered. She had three children before the marriage broke up.

When, she came across Freud's book on the interpretation of dreams in 1910, Melanie Klein knew she wanted to practice psychoanalysis herself. She continued undergoing the analysis she had started with Ferenczi with another psychologist, Karl Abraham (1877–1925), who, like Ferenczi, encouraged her to work with children. But it was Ernest Jones, who had by then formed the British Analytical Society, who persuaded her to leave Berlin, where she had begun her pioneering work, and come to England to practice in London.

As child analysis was relatively uncharted territory, Klein had to start almost from scratch. She found that watching very young children at play, and taking an interest in what they were doing, could be very revealing. She developed "play therapy" to explore their unconscious motivation as they displayed their feelings, fantasies, and anxieties through the ways they treated toys and used modelling materials such as plasticine—a kind of childhood equivalent of free association.

Klein reached some conclusions that were at odds with the Freudian stages of development. Her assessments indicated that Oedipal feelings in both boys and girls towards their parental opposites were built in, and that the super-ego, the capacity for moral behaviour, was in evidence even when the child was only two years old.

Going back to the very beginning of life, Klein developed the concept of "object relations", whereby the child first latches onto things, rather than people. Thus the baby first sees the breast that feeds her as an independent object and doesn't associate it with its owner since it doesn't have the capacity to process a complete entity like a "mother". Klein suggested that a baby's pursuit of survival generates two conflicting notions: love and hate. She finds herself in a world that has the capacity both to satisfy and to frustrate. If she is hungry, she becomes anxious, as there is no certainty, within her limited experience, that she will be fed.

So the child's inner world is primarily defensive, protecting the self from an environment of discomfort, pain, and frustration. This unstable and primitive mode of identification was termed by Klein "the paranoid-schizoid position". The infant needs everything; he can spare nothing. But then others around him will surely be the same. So he has to develop the capacity not to be overly dependent. Part of him hates the mother for the power she has. If the mother withholds anything from the child, then she must be keeping it for herself. Klein held that the baby wants to destroy the mother so what he can't have, no one else can either. On top of all this, she factored in the Oedipal fantasies: the child's desire for his mother, and the perceived rivalry from the father, who takes the mother's care and attention away from him.

However, the time arrives when the child is able to realize that "mother" is a whole person; the mother he hates is also the mother he loves. The need to preserve this entity constrains the instinctive impulse to attack. In the background is the fear of rejection—what Klein called "the depressive position"—as well might be the case as the poor mite realizes that nothing is ever going to be easy or straightforward in life!

Another process also takes place, which Klein termed "introjection". In this, an infant, in trying to make himself acceptable to the mother, seeks to adopt her values and rid himself of his less desirable traits. Acceptance of her as she is encourages acceptance of himself, and, ideally, this gradually leads to a more integrated person. But the sense of responsibility in the child brought about by the depressive position can also be an appalling burden if he is made accountable for events outside his control. If his parents quarrel or if he feels unwanted, he construes it as being his fault. Threats not to love him if he disobeys, or implying that he is responsible for a parent's illness or death, may shatter the frail structure of early development. Sadly, the counselling assessment often reveals that the client has endured just such situations in childhood.

Two major ideas have since contributed to and expanded on Klein's work: John Bowlby's (1907–1990) theory of attachment and Donald Winnicott's (1896–1971) concept of the "good enough" mother.

John Bowlby was monitored by Melanie Klein when he was training as a psychoanalyst. But whereas Klein held that children's emotional problems were largely due to fantasies stemming from conflicts between aggression and sexual drives, Bowlby proposed that children come into the world pre-programmed to form attachments with others, because this will help them to survive. Whilst the child may relate preferentially to one parent, Bowlby took the view that the combination of mother and father produces much healthier and more productive attachment than from one parent alone. Contrary to the Freudian view of fathers being perceived as threats by their sons, Bowlby saw fathers as playing a vital role in providing stimulation outside the home, and encouraging boys to extend their life experience. The absence of this constructive environment often results in emotional difficulties for the child. Missing the security and anchoring of attachment in childhood, young people may lose a sense of who they are and drift into delinquency. A number of surveys have shown that the children of split parents are more likely to have behavioural problems.

The benefits of a child's confident attachment are evident from the earliest days. The infant runs ahead of her parents, looking over her shoulder to make sure that she's been noticed. She scampers further until she is called back. She has satisfied her need for the beginnings of independence but with the certainty that she will still be protected. The young child goes out to explore and take risks, knowing that when he returns home he can share his experiences, learn from mistakes, and be reassured if scared.

It is important to distinguish attachment from dependency. Dependency means that the child cannot function normally in the absence of the person to whom they have attached.

The impact on the child when attachment is withdrawn is sometimes seen when a mother has had to spend time in hospital. Typically, when the mother comes home, the child first of all ignores her, then clings tightly to her, and then gets angry with her for threatening his security, fearful of it happening again. But social attitudes also play a role. Not so very long ago, many children went to boarding school from as young as five or six. The sounds of crying and quiet misery after lights out on the first night were considered quite normal as evidence of "homesickness".

It can be seen that a considerable burden falls on the parents to guide the child productively through these life processes. Bowlby recognized that being a parent is very hard work, not so much the actual caring as the unrelenting day-to-day pressure to keep it up. He deemed that parents need support as well, and whatever may currently be considered socially acceptable, this was not a job for a woman on her own; single mothers are disadvantaged by their reduced likelihood of getting the assistance that they need.

Lack of attachment in early years can lead to reluctance to form relationships in later life for fear of abandonment.

Karen came for counselling because she was becoming impatient with herself and "wanted to move on". Her history revealed that she had been the eldest of two sisters but always felt her mother preferred her sibling. She related better to her father, but when she was seven he told her he wasn't her real parent. Karen was deeply shocked and felt that she could henceforth trust nothing her mother or, as she now knew him, her step-father, said to her. She could recall few details of her childhood, having, as she put it, "blanked it out". But from being an organized and tidy child she started skipping school and generally behaving in an anti-social way.

Eventually, when she was nine, after persistent nagging, her mother reluctantly took her to see her real father whom Karen learned had walked out on her mother before she was born. The occasion was not a success. Her biological father had remarried and his present wife was not well disposed towards her. At this point, Karen made the largely unconscious decision that in the absence of anyone else she could rely on, she had to take care of herself.

She started seriously working at school, won herself a scholarship, left home, and took a job in public relations where she performed very well. Her progress was partly driven by the belief that she had to be outstanding in at least one measurable respect to be worthwhile.

Karen's imbued sense of rejection made her reluctant to put herself in a position where she might be rejected again, so she was reluctant to take the risk of having boyfriends.

Karen was having to deal with two issues: rejection by her father, and to some extent her mother, and the consequential experience of loss. No one wants to believe that they have no place in the world, no value. So Karen had to try to create a value for herself, which she did at work. Her understanding of the factors that led her to adopt the beliefs she had about herself enabled her to develop the emotional insight to work towards self-acceptance and the freedom to be truly herself. This was not a quick resolution, but a gradual process of recovery.

Girls who have experienced detached parenting will sometimes have huge families and ensure that their children attach to them by indulging them to the extent that they may later be ill-equipped to face the outside world.

The breaking of attachment often leads to difficulties with confidence and self-acceptance. This was the case with Paul who wanted to—indeed, knew he had to—control his anger in order to preserve his marriage. He recalled feeling happy in his early childhood. He was close to and felt protected by his mother, although he was aware that his father was a jealous man and had wanted a daughter rather than a son. When he was five years old, Paul overheard him shout at his mother: "It's either him or me; make up your mind!" Although he didn't hear his mother's response, and never asked her about it, he felt that she was thereafter more circumspect in her affection towards him. This made him uncertain and fearful.

When he was eleven, his father turned up at a football game in which Paul scored three goals, but missed one at the end of the match. He heard his father comment: "What a wimp!" Paul was hugely angry and, determined to prove his worth, started to work hard at school. He got good O levels and wanted to sit his A levels, but his father said it would be a waste of time. Paul left home as soon as he could and joined a manufacturing company. At the time he came for counselling he had moved up to manager and was on a good salary, probably earning more than his father.

This background information didn't emerge immediately as Paul hadn't recognized its significance. He had felt his success in business had closed that chapter of conflict with his father. He was married now and had a three year-old daughter but found himself competing for her attention, which annoyed him. He would lose his temper at the slightest hint of criticism from his wife who was understandably becoming fed up with having endlessly to pick her words so he wouldn't take offence. This, too, irritated him, as he realized what was happening and felt he should be above this. He didn't have these problems at work and was somewhat bewildered as to why he should be like he was at home. What else did he have to prove?

A major step forward for Paul was an understanding of how negative events in early life can programme a way of thinking that is difficult to alter. As with Karen, his childhood experience led him to believe that he could not tolerate the risk of being rejected again. So he over-reacted to any negative comment directed at him. But he recognized that in demanding that he be shown constant affection, he was putting his wife in an impossible position. His strength lay in being able to use his new understanding to create a more realistic perspective on life events and provide a secure environment for his family.

* * *

Donald Winnicott (1896–1971) was a paediatrician, so he tended to see very young children in the company of their mothers. Like Melanie Klein, he watched them at play but focused particularly on their interaction with the mother as a means of assessing their development. He asserted that the baby should be considered not in isolation, but as a part of a nursing couple. He meant by this that for the child to realize its potential, the mother needed to provide focused and directed maternal care. Care in this context is much more than just seeing that the baby's physical needs for survival are met; it means providing the necessary tuition to help it towards growth and independence. Winnicott coined the phrase "a good enough mother", not as a palliative to excuse ineffectual parenting, but to define the tricky process of adapting to the baby's overall needs as it matures from a creature of blind dependency to becoming a whole being.

In the beginning, the mother's task is to provide a totally reliable "holding environment", meeting the baby's every demand and allowing it a temporary illusion of omnipotence. The baby is not grateful; it treats its mother like a slave and tolerates no failure to give it what it wants. A critical ability for the mother at this stage is to be able to accept and survive this onslaught with equanimity.

So it could be said that at the very outset the mother *is* perfect. Nothing is too much trouble, no sacrifice in sleep or personal time too great. Gradually, however, she adopts the "good enough" role; she continues providing what the infant needs, but leaves a time lag between the demands and their satisfaction and progressively extends that lag. The child does not like being thwarted of instant gratification, but begins to acquire a sense of reality, increasingly seeing the mother as an independent person, which, in turn encourages him to recognize independence in himself. Winnicott made the point that the trick of being a "good enough mother" is to give the child a sense of loosening, rather than the shock of being dropped. The infant's recognition that he has a personality, with options of how to think and act, can be quite taxing, and babies may find this responsibility difficult to cope with. This is much like the depressive position described by Melanie Klein. The young child has to start taking decisions and distinguishing between what he is and what he is not, which expectations are realistic and which are not.

Problems can arise if, instead of providing a constructive environment, the mother starts to project her own problems onto the child. In order to try to accommodate her within his very limited means, the infant starts to adopt a false self to please her and meet her expectations, thereby protecting himself from pain and rejection. If the requirement to comply or imitate is too great, the child begins to confuse the person that he really is with the one that he is being obliged to be. In this way, the infant may completely conceal his true self behind the false front he has had to develop. Of course, in a civilized society, we often do have to put on a false front, observing the rules of good behaviour even when we're feeling ill-tempered. But if we cannot be ourselves within ourselves and with those closest to us, then we may create a not wholly knowable person, somehow lacking a focus.

The American sociologist, Morris Massey (1939–), neatly defines three phases of development from infancy through childhood and adolescence.

The first of these, the imprint stage, takes us up to the age of seven. During this period, we absorb everything around us, accepting much of it as true, especially when it comes from our parents. This is the time when we should be able to develop a sense of right and wrong, good and bad.

Next comes the modelling period. From the ages of eight to thirteen we copy people, often our parents, but others as well. Rather than blind acceptance, we tend to test ideas out for ourselves to see how they fit. This is a time when we may want to assess our skills, and be prepared to take risks in so doing.

Finally, there is the socializing phase, from thirteen to twenty-one, when we are largely influenced by our peers. As we develop as individuals, we naturally turn to people who seem like us. We may join a gang or a group of like-minded contemporaries, perhaps adopting certain rituals, a form of vocabulary, or a particular way of speaking to give ourselves a shared identity. Other impacting factors include the media, and especially websites, that seem to resonate with the values of our peers.

The steep learning process of the very young child needs to be nurtured by close contact with the parents. Not so very long ago most children were raised in an environment in which the whole family assembled at meal times, which were often a forum for lively debate. Being read a bedtime story was a major event in the day. Watching television, going for walks, and playing games would also be family activities.

However, family meal times are now largely history and in many households the formal dining room has been converted for some other use. Children as young as four or five are exposed to the artificial world of computer games, sometimes for long periods. Alarm was recently raised in America when a three year-old, whose mother left him to spend five hours a day in front of the television, was reduced to parroting lines from cartoon characters and could do nothing else.

Health and Safety has become something of an oxymoron, with obsessions about the avoidance of any kind of risk arguably having a negative impact on children's health. Massey's modelling period has been corrupted by legislation that forbids children from playing conkers or flying paper aeroplanes because the activities are deemed too dangerous—a nanny state run amok. Children are now much less likely to be allowed to set out unsupervised to explore, climb trees, go cycling, visit the local shops, or experience other adventures that are a vital part of growing up. One of the saddest ironies is that because children are not permitted to play out of doors or out of adult sight in case they harm themselves or become subject to an unwelcome advance, they may spend more time on the computer in their bedrooms where they are vulnerable to on-line predation.

This is not intended as a yearning for a mythically halcyon age. No one would want to return to the time when children were "seen but not heard". But it is true to say that a significant number of people seeking help through counselling have endured childhood trauma of some kind which has left them feeling inadequate or uncertain as to who they are or how they are supposed to be. For the many who have grown up free to make their own mistakes and learn from them, the current environment may seem far from ideal.

* * *

So, in summary: From the somewhat remote on-the-couch free association, we have moved to a more personal approach, with therapist and client sitting face to face. Disciplines have been put in place for therapy to be conducted within a manageable framework. From an authoritarian position, where only the analyst can interpret what is going on, we have graduated to one in which the patient is shown respect and encouraged to make his or her own contribution to the sessions.

Valuable work has been done to achieve an understanding of the factors that influence the early years. Whatever the reason people may come for counselling it might seem that the requirements for addressing a person's difficulties and conducting effective therapy are in place.

But one man had different ideas. His name was Carl Rogers.

CHAPTER FOUR

The road to self-discovery

Oak Park, Chicago was the birthplace of Carl Rogers (1902–1987), still one of the most influential figures in psychotherapy today. Rogers pioneered a move away from traditional methodologies. In contrast to Freud's rather gloomy view of human nature as a cauldron of sexuality and aggressive tendencies, manifested in the id and the ego, which the super-ego struggled to keep under control, Rogers took a very different view of humanity. Perhaps because for a time he studied to be a priest, he saw people as fundamentally healthy and believed that we all have the ability to develop our potential to the fullest extent, provided that conditions are in place for us to do so.

A plant trying to grow in a dim and musty cellar will send out tendrils towards the light it needs If it is to survive. But, significantly, if the plant is moved and placed in an environment conducive to healthy growth it will automatically thrive. This is the essence of Rogers' therapeutic approach. He was intrigued by the way that even if conditions are harsh, this tendency will endow the organism with the capacity to make the very best of what is available to sustain itself. Thus, mushrooms can push up paving stones, birds migrate for thousands of miles, and humans can create works of art, utilize atomic energy, and invent the cuckoo clock.

Rogers was suspicious of the psychoanalytical techniques of suggestion, direction, and persuasion to effect changes in the patient based on pre-conceived criteria for mental health. Instead, he held that human problems were distortions created by our perceptions of what is required of us. Our parents, schoolteachers, peers, and the media, all seek to impose upon us conditions of worth. This can give rise to conditional self-acceptance in that we base our self-esteem on the standards others impose on us, rather than being ourselves. The more that society is at odds with how we may instinctively see ourselves, as opposed to what we perceive we ought to be, the greater the incongruity and levels of anger, anxiety, depression, or other forms of distress we may experience. In this respect, the Rogerian approach also recognizes that childhood events can significantly affect the way we view things in later life.

So, this is not just a matter of morality, being good or bad. As individuals, we are all of us sometimes negatively influenced by situations or events that other people seem to have no problem with. Why do some people feel that if someone dislikes them there must be something wrong with them, while others do not? Or seem dedicated to putting other people's interests first to the detriment of their own? Or feel that if they fail at any one task, they must be a failure?

Rogers took the view that only the person concerned had the key to what was inhibiting the process he called "self-actualization"; it was only the individual who had the inner resources to effect the necessary actions to achieve it. The therapist's task was to facilitate this process. As Rogers saw it, this meant, effectively, changing from an idea of "How can I treat or cure this person?" to "How can I provide a relationship which enables this person to treat or cure themselves?"

You will have been aware that in the previous chapters all those undergoing therapy were invariably referred to as "patients" in recognition of the premise that they were deemed to be ill. It was Rogers who described people coming to him as "clients"—the term used in counselling today. In this way, he accorded the person the status of one making a choice to seek a resolution to problems, rather than being obliged to submit themselves to authoritarian instructions, however well intended.

Rogers realized that to be an effective therapist he had to be able to experience a deep understanding of the client's subjective world and ensure that the client was aware of this understanding. He specified the essential conditions needed to create a productive environment. The therapist has to be genuine, empathic, and non-judgemental, and has to have for the client unconditional positive regard. For the clients, this experience of total acceptance is essential to enable them to build the confidence they may have been lacking to truly be themselves. The argument is that if the therapist can accept them, why should they not accept themselves? Rogerian therapy is often termed "person-centred". But since all counselling is, by definition, person-centred, this seems an oddly tautological description.

On the face of it, meeting the criteria for the Rogerian approach might seem relatively straightforward. Being warm and friendly to your clients, listening sympathetically to what they have to say without imposing your own views or allowing your prejudices to intrude, should surely be standard practice in any counselling relationship. But the reality is much subtler than this. Rogerian therapy is about creating the climate for positive change.

Let's look more closely at the "essential conditions", all of which are closely interlinked. First, what do we mean by "genuine"? Being genuine may be defined as counsellors being true to themselves, transparent, self-accepting, and acknowledging their humanity in all its aspects. As such, they will not seek to hide behind professional defences nor impose strictures on how their clients present themselves. This state of rapport between the counsellor's inner self and their outer self is termed "congruence".

If we set out to buy something, say a computer, where we may need help or advice, accomplished salespersons will give us their full attention without being distracted by what is going on around them. They will take an informed interest in our needs, help us make the best choice, and not laugh at us if we betray our ignorance of how the equipment works. In this environment, we are likely to feel that they can be trusted and be willing to follow their advice. These same salespersons may vary their approach or use different language with other customers according to how they present themselves and their perceived level of knowledge.

But for all their solicitousness, they are not being genuine in the therapeutic sense. They operate behind a façade that limits the extent to which they will accept us. If we represent a type of person they do not like, if we are abrupt or seem not to be respecting their authority, they will probably react quite swiftly and want to terminate the discussion or call someone else over to deal with us. Of course, for our part in this situation we don't expect unlimited tolerance, especially if we are rude or abusive, and thus we adapt our approach accordingly.

The individuals coming for counselling, whose experience of people's behaviour has left them feeling compromised, may be instinctively distrustful, believing that others will always first pursue their own interests, possibly employing flattery in order to get their way. But if they find in the counsellor someone whom they perceive as being genuine, that is, open and honest, and with no hidden agenda that might warp their responses, they may be willing to suspend their caution. This, too, produces congruence where both parties are in accord, so helping to break down the barriers that would inhibit issues from being discussed freely. In the safe environment that has been created, the client can feel secure and the counsellor can be open in their responses—asking questions if seeking clarification, being spontaneous, and responding with vigour if the need arises, whilst still being supportive.

Empathy, the second essential condition, should not be confused with sympathy. If a friend tells you a relationship has fallen through or he's lost his job you may well feel sympathy for him without needing to have the full facts of the situation. Empathy is about active, focused understanding: understanding the other person's point of view, his circumstances, thoughts, and feelings. It means stepping into his shoes, seeing things as he does. We've all of us on occasion been frustrated by someone to whom we are trying to explain our feelings about a situation, but who simply doesn't seem to "get it". The other person may truly want to help, but because his disposition is different to ours there is simply no way of our getting through to him. So we have to let it go, and a discussion that in other circumstances might have had a productive outcome, falters and dies.

But the Rogerian approach is that if we can truly enter and understand a person's subjective world, we can break this deadlock and demonstrate that we are in tune with them. For those who may be in despair that they will ever be understood, having at last someone who can relate to their difficulties and make sense of them can be hugely restorative.

Being non-judgemental, the next Rogerian "essential", is not about refraining from having opinions or views about a client or pretending that bad behaviour or malign thoughts are other than what they are. But if a client is being held back by irrational ideas about how they or the world should be, the counsellor needs to be able to engage with them without allowing their own prejudices (because, of course, we all have them) to intrude, since this would risk distorting or compromising their response.

Closely linked to this is unconditional positive regard. Conditional regard, even if positive, depends on the client meeting certain criteria that the therapist might impose, even if only instinctively. That regard may falter if these conditions are not met. Regard that is unconditional means valuing the client, even whilst knowing her failings. It is also important that the client knows the therapist knows of her failings and is not put off by them. In this environment the client feels confident to explore her thoughts and feelings, positive or negative, without danger of rejection or condemnation.

It would be wrong to give the impression that unconditional positive regard means that the Rogerian therapist would find it acceptable if the client indicated she intended to harm herself or another person, or that the therapist would endorse cruelty or extreme selfishness. But an understanding of human fallibility without condemning it enables the counsellor to work with the client from a constructive standpoint.

Rogers was also concerned with detecting incongruity, a lack of rapport within parts of the individual. You may recall that Winnicott identified a situation in which the infant may suppress his natural behaviour and characteristics in order to comply with a mother who saddles him with her own problems. The child adopts a "false self" to please her and meet her expectations. Aspects of such a false self can continue into adulthood and so compromise who the person really is. Rogers used a technique he called "reflection". Reflection can be described as the way in which counsellors use their clients' words or the context in which they are spoken to feed back to them their recognition of what the client wants to convey. This not only helps consolidate the relationship between client and counsellor, it may also move the whole process of exploration forward, as the client feels able to continue without the distraction of worrying about whether she has been understood and accepted.

Reflection has the further benefit of enabling the individual to recognize when he may have adopted an exaggerated response to a situation or where there are inconsistencies in his thinking. For example, a client, David, makes a statement, seemingly between gritted teeth: "I absolutely have to get through my accountancy exam." The therapist reflects that being a successful accountant is very important to him. But hearing his words played back to him, David adopts a defensive stance: "Well, if I'm to make a decent living, I've got to, haven't I?" The therapist may reflect the idea that this is something David has to do but may also invite him to define "a decent living".

In the accepting and unthreatening environment in which he finds himself, David may at that moment acknowledge a truth he has never dared to express before, which is that he knows he doesn't have the right temperament to be an accountant, and that there is more to "a decent living" than how much he earns. In his heart, he would like to be an ecologist working with museums, but his father has impressed upon him that it would be irresponsible to pursue this as there is little money in it. David knows that if he gets his degree he will have to follow a career as an accountant. This is really the dichotomy that has brought him to counselling, rather than just anxiety about passing an exam.

Part of him wants to sabotage his prospects by failing deliberately, but if he doesn't pass, his father will be appalled. David rather hopes the therapist will help solve the problem for him by giving him advice, but this would run completely counter to the whole purpose of Rogerian therapy, or indeed any form of counselling. Only the client can determine what is in their best interests as a fully functioning individual. David may well decide that in an uncertain world, financial security has to take precedence. Or he could follow his instincts and become an ecologist, recognizing that life might in some respects be harder, but being prepared to accept this. If his father decides to be upset by his choice then that's unfortunate, but down to him. Whatever action David takes it will be his decision, not one imposed upon him from outside. This is the essence of self-actualization—being who we actually are, rather than who it is deemed we should be.

Bear in mind, from all the above, that what we're looking at in the context of this book is a philosophy—a basis for conducting counselling rather than instruction on how to be a counsellor. On the face of it, a modality that is not bound by the rules of a specific theory may seem attractive and accessible. Following on perhaps from Florence Nightingale's edict that the first requirement of treatment is that it should do no harm, a person-centred approach is likely to be the new student's introduction to counselling. But acquiring the skills of unconditional positive regard, empathy, and genuineness and, importantly, holding onto them throughout the period of counselling, can be achieved only through practice and training. Rogers developed this approach over many years of clinical work.

It can be readily imagined that transference and countertransference could run riot in this environment. Clients who feel that their counsellor is the first person who totally accepts them may be extremely reluctant to terminate therapy. So, far from moving towards self-actualization, there is a risk they will become very dependent—exactly the opposite of what is intended. So the productive management of transference constitutes an important part of the training. Leading Rogerian therapists have expressed concern at the way that some counsellors, without properly understanding the full implications, claim to use a person-centred approach as a springboard into their own methodology, so greatly oversimplifying a demanding and highly disciplined way of working.

An effective way of understanding a therapeutic approach is to see an experienced practitioner at work. In 1964, Dr Everett Shostrom, a psychologist from California, made an educational film entitled *Three Approaches to Psychotherapy* in which a thirty year-old, recently divorced woman called Gloria, engages in half-hour sessions with three therapists, each working from a different orientation. It was a clever idea and the first time complete therapy sessions had been filmed, albeit in shortened form. The session with Carl Rogers works well in demonstrating the effectiveness of his approach when both therapist and client are focused on enabling the client to move forward.

Gloria first presents her problem. She has been asked by Pammy, her rather precocious nine-year-old daughter, if she has had sex with anyone since the divorce. Although Gloria has had other relationships, she assured her daughter that she had not. Now she is torn between telling Pammy the truth and risking her disapproval, or not telling her and feeling dishonest. If she does tell her daughter, or, worse, if Pammy discovers the deception, Gloria fears that the child will distrust her thereafter. She says she wants to feel comfortable with whatever she does.

If you see the film, which, fortunately, is available on YouTube, observe how Rogers "reflects". He doesn't parrot her words, but ensures she recognizes that he fully empathizes with the dilemma she is presenting, without presuming to advise her on what to do. At one point, Gloria gets quite cross and tells Rogers she feels he is "just letting her stew in her difficulty". She demands that he help her get rid of her guilt. Rogers tells her that it would be impertinent of him to solve this for her but that he would like to help her solve it for herself—the essence of leading the client towards self-actualization.

Gloria goes on to say that if she met a man she truly loved and respected that would be fine, but she likes to have sex for the pleasure of it. Watch how Rogers keeps her on track, and how she starts to work things out for herself, defining the issues that need to be addressed. Rogers suggests that she resents the dilemma that her daughter has unconsciously imposed on her. Once again, Gloria asks for a solution. Rogers apologizes for seeming to be evasive but suggests that the problem is that she is not being honest with herself.

At this point, Gloria realizes that the real work lies in her being genuine, and thus grasps the fact that, to some extent, she has to be her own counsellor. She asks Rogers where she should start. Again, he doesn't offer her advice but empathizes with her that she is taking a chance. Gloria says she needs someone to push her and Rogers offers her a life-line, proposing that she ask herself what is the value of someone's love if it is based on a false premise. At this point, Gloria takes another important step, recognizing that the way forward is to accept herself, and hope that her daughter will accept her, too. But she knows she cannot demand this. Life is risk and responsibility. It is the freedom to choose that enables us to focus on our priorities.

It is notable how completely Rogers is at peace with himself. He is not smug, nor does he pretend to know all the answers. His reflection comes across as spontaneous and not driven by dogma or a fixed set of criteria.

An important factor impacting on an individual reaching their full potential is the nature and intensity of events taking place in their lives. As we have seen, the search for self-actualization is driven by unsatisfied needs. Satisfying our needs (rather than wants) is the means whereby we can move ourselves towards this goal. But these needs can only be met if the person is in a condition to address them. We might reasonably assume from the way Gloria presents herself, well groomed and smartly turned out, that she was not immediately concerned with survival. But if she was in a struggle, say, to save her house from being repossessed because she was behind with her mortgage payments, it is unlikely she would be in a frame of mind to address the subtleties of her relationship with her daughter, however beneficial this might be. Her overwhelming priority in this situation would be to secure her home. An understanding of the factors that may incapacitate a client's drive to be fully themselves is an important part of the therapist's work.

A theory of the issues influencing human motivation was developed by the psychologist Abraham Maslow (1908–1970), who defined what he called a "Hierarchy of Needs". This acknowledges the Rogerian concept that all humans have within them the capacity for self-actualization, but stipulates that lower needs have to be satisfied before those higher up the scale can be addressed. Maslow broke these needs down into five levels, often represented as a pyramid.

The lowest level, the fifth, constitutes meeting the basic requirements for survival: air, water, food, and some kind of shelter. The water may not be clean, the shelter no more than a piece of tarpaulin, and food scrounged from rubbish tips, so long as it enables the person to stay alive.

Once this basic state has been achieved, the individual is motivated to move up to level four. Now the aim is more long term. She looks for safety and continuity: a home that offers reliable protection from the elements in secure surroundings, and a decent living that ensures her position at this level can be sustained.

With these needs met, she is equipped to climb to level three. Now she seeks to fulfil her social needs: to enter into a loving relationship, start a family, make friends, and be a part of a like-minded cultural group.

The individual next strives to attain level two. Here she seeks status: to be accepted and valued by others in the community. The desire for this is logical enough, and achieving it confers an extra level of security. There is a danger here, however. If the individual feels she's not reaching the level of recognition she tells herself she must have, she may struggle to please those around her or become a bully in order to acquire approval and respect—an exhausting process as there is, of course, no certainty that others will ever oblige her in this regard.

The top level, the peak of the pyramid, represents the person's full capacity for self-actualization. She is spontaneous, natural, objective, creative, inventive, and accepting of herself without being complacent. In this state, she is willing to learn from experience, not be dependent on others for her self-worth, and is interested in reaching her full potential without making unrealistic demands of herself. We can probably none of us achieve this dizzy height full-time or on all occasions, but being aware of the rewards it brings makes it a goal worth striving for.

This final stage is the one that both David, the client whom we visited earlier, and Gloria aspired to reach. David realized he was basing his worth on his father's approval, so obliging him to pursue a career in which he had little interest. He knew that if he did not go through with his exams, his father would be scathingly angry. But he realized that he had to take control of his own destiny and work towards self-actualization. This would mean accepting himself, taking the risk of making mistakes, and, if they occurred, being prepared to learn from them.

Unlike David, the difficulty for Gloria was that in the present situation she had the esteem she wanted. Her problem was that she knew this esteem was supported by a lie. She was by no means sure how her daughter would respond if she told her the truth. She very much hoped that Pammy would accept her but recognized that what was even more important was that she accept herself.

Maslow's Hierarchy of Needs is a useful concept, but should not be interpreted too rigidly. There are many people around the world who, by some standards, are living in extraordinarily straitened circumstances. They may find it difficult to satisfy the needs of even the lowest level, but in terms of relationships and having status within their communities, they may be much further up the scale and, despite their disadvantaged state, may move on to self-fulfilment. Equally, there are those whose wealth and achievements easily qualify them to reach the highest level but who seem never able to satisfy their need for esteem no matter how big their yachts, as they will measure success only by comparison with people they have identified as being in competition with them.

The client who seems to be stuck at a particular level may be fearful of taking the next step up in case she runs into difficulties. But Maslow took the view that if you deliberately plan on being less than you are capable of, then you'll be unhappy for the rest of your life.

It is probable that the would-be person-centred counsellor will be especially attracted by the dynamics of the human personality and the value of understanding a client's problems experienced from their viewpoint. The counsellor may be less interested in following a structured theory than in drawing out the inner resources of their clients to enable them to be themselves in the full sense, and so create an environment in which they can pursue their lives with confidence.

That said, Rogers' core conditions of non-judgemental positive regard, congruence, and empathy are immensely important irrespective of how the therapist chooses to practice.

* * *

All counselling approaches depend on the therapist being able to share an understanding of their clients' presentations and the reasons they may be thinking or acting in a particular way. But this can be very challenging because there are no rules as to how someone should respond to a difficulty she may be experiencing, or standard criteria as to how she may be expected to feel or behave.

In the following chapter we'll explore the approach of two practitioners, who, like Rogers, had the goal of enabling their clients to make sense of their world and their place in it, and from there to be able to develop the capability of assuming authority over their lives.

CHAPTER FIVE

How we construct our world

In physical medicine the diagnosis of a set of symptoms will usually point to a particular disorder. Unfortunately, psychotherapy offers no such straightforward process. In an attempt to create some set of ground rules, many of the pioneers drew up charts of how we could be expected to think and act at different periods of our lives. Bowlby and Winnicott explored mainly evolution in the early years. Jung developed the idea of four stages of development and consciousness from childhood through youth, middle life, and old age. The Danish psychoanalyst, Eric Erikson (1902–1994), later created his psychosocial theory, The Eight Stages of Man—our psychological development from birth to the end of our lives. Daniel Levinson (1920–), an American psychiatrist, came up with a hypothesis in which he predicted that the pattern of an individual's progress at any given point in time will be the product of their social and physical environment. In this, he distinguished between men and women in two books, *The Seasons of a Man's Life* (1978) and *The Seasons of a Woman's Life* (1996).

Following somewhat along this same predictive path, the American Psychiatric Association (APA) developed a *Diagnostic and Statistical Manual* (*DSM*) which sets out to identify all the characteristics of a range of mental health disorders and optimal treatment approaches. The current model is *DSM-IV* with *DSM-V* on the way. The *DSM* is regarded as a bible by many of those making psychiatric diagnoses in the United States and in other countries as well. But the APA warns that there should be no assumption that each category of mental disorder is a discrete entity with absolute boundaries. So even the *DSM* is not a perfect diagnostic tool.

So how do we "read" our clients? How do they read themselves? And, equally important of course, as counsellors, how do we read *our*selves? These were questions that intrigued an American psychologist, George Kelly (1905–1967). Kelly took his degree in physics and mathematics before training as a Freudian psychoanalyst, obtaining a PhD in 1931. Because he practised in Kansas, he saw mostly people in the farming community. He would listen to what his patients had to say and offer them interpretations of their dreams in accordance with psychoanalytical practice. But it began to occur to him that too often he was making assumptions about the derivation of their difficulties without really understanding enough about their culture, or factoring in sufficiently what they thought might be the reasons that they were feeling anxious and/or depressed.

As with Freud, Kelly's background and training directed him to approach therapy from a scientific standpoint. He formulated the idea of humans as scientists constantly forming and testing hypotheses to make sense of their environment, with the objective of enabling them to anticipate events and respond to them productively. He saw this process starting from earliest childhood as we gather the materials with which to build our lives. Our concepts, or "constructs", as Kelly called them, have two elements: first, the template we have built from our experience to date, and second the way we draw on this experience to think and act in our best interests, as we interpret them. Kelly called his theory "personal construct psychology". He did not go along with classification systems or ideas of personality types, arguing that since everyone has different experiences, everyone's construction of reality is different.

Those who have worked in, or have had dealings with, any organization which sets out to offer advice or provide information will soon recognize that the people there do not treat every enquiry in the same way, even if there are set rules for dealing with particular situations. The assessment of a problem, and the attitude towards the enquirer, will reflect the individual's construct of what is acceptable as difficult or worthy of particular attention.

We do not, of course, exist in isolation; our behaviour and views on life reflect those of people to whom we relate. Kelly recognized this. As a part of his assessment process he used a series of grids as diagnostic tools. He would then ask his clients to define aspects of their constructs and compare these with the constructs of people close to them, such as work colleagues and members of their family, or those people whose characteristics aroused strong emotions in them. This process allows both therapist and client to create a picture of the client's inner view of reality and define where there may be anomalies or contradictions.

The essence of constructs is that they can be adapted and reconstructed if the evidence shows that the original construct is questionable. So if, for example, you decide to go out for dinner at a pub and you have a vile meal, you won't go there again. You might, nevertheless, try eating out at another pub. But if you have a further unsatisfactory culinary experience, you may well decide to avoid eating in pubs altogether. This is your experiential construct. However, a friend later persuades you, against your better judgement, to come for supper at his local, which he swears serves the best nosh for miles around. To your surprise, you find that he is right. So not all pubs serve up rubbishy food. On this basis, you "reconstruct" to accommodate the new information you now have. In future, you might go for dinner at an inn, but you'll be sure to check the *Good Pub Guide* first.

This is a simple illustration, but Kelly's theory extends to the recognition of a range of factors, or corollaries, which follow on from an initial construct, and which influence a decision as to whether that construct should be retained, modified, or, in extremis, abandoned. These include the person's thoughts, feelings, and experiences, the choices available, and the social implications of change. Kelly also identified "core constructs", that is, the deeply held values and principles that we are reluctant to change even when we are faced with information that may seem to invalidate them. Our ideas of what is important or morally wrong can have far-reaching consequences.

As an example, Ian wanted help because he was having serious concerns about the state of his marriage. After he and his first wife had divorced, he married Elaine, also divorced, who had two sons aged eleven and thirteen. As a child, Ian and his two brothers had been brought up in an authoritarian household in which they were expected to show due deference to their "elders and betters". Ian felt that Elaine's boys were far too casual in the way that they behaved towards him. He would order them to keep their rooms tidy and expect them to change their ways if he commented adversely on their table manners or the way they dressed, but they responded only half-heartedly, if at all. This resulted in major rows. But Ian stuck with his construct, which was that children, boys especially, are bound always to show respect to a father-figure. This was how the world should work; otherwise it would all end in anarchy. He had no fall-back position. What he found particularly galling was that Elaine didn't seem too bothered about the boys' laid-back attitude.

In the counselling room he resisted the suggestion that not everyone in his position would experience his level of anger and bewilderment. He said that what other people did was up to them. He was not prepared to abandon a construct on which he had based a large part of his moral code. But he later came to recognize that the conditions on which his original construct was based (effectively, an unwritten agreement within his own family) did not necessarily apply in every situation and that the boys' casualness was more likely to be a reflection of an upbringing very different to his own, rather than a sign of disrespect towards him. With this in mind, Ian felt able to adopt a less aggressive approach to discipline. Interestingly, when he stepped back, he found that his wife, who had clearly abided by the maxim "Don't bark if you have a dog", started to take up some of the work of disciplining her sons.

The feeling of being unable to live up to a self-evidently sound construct can be extremely distressing. John was a priest who came for counselling because he was appalled to find that when he was giving a sermon, profanities kept slipping into his mind and he was fearful of saying them aloud, although he had never done so. How could a man dedicated to the priesthood possibly have such obscene thoughts? Feeling himself almost beyond redemption, he tried to neutralize his thinking by shouting the offending words when on his own until he felt bored and exhausted, but to no effect.

John was able to accept that there was nothing inherently wicked about experiencing unwanted thoughts. He did not act on them and, as such, remained in command of the situation. In due course, he recalled a time when he had had to deliver an important address when he was unwell. He came to recognize that he was substituting his fear of giving an imperfect sermon with a fear of swearing which now became the focus of his anxiety. John realized he was making a rod for his own back by insisting that everything delivered from the pulpit had to be perfect. He was encouraged to accept that, whilst he would naturally wish to give of his best, there would inevitably be times when he did not meet his desired standards. By taking the pressure off himself by acknowledging his own human frailty his anxiety started to abate, and with it his fear of using bad language.

We sometimes maintain a construct which we believe reflects a true state of affairs and must therefore be inevitable. This was the case with Olive, a young client who was in despair of ever finding a partner. Three relationships in succession had foundered for unconnected reasons, but she had come to the conclusion that there must be something wrong with her. With this construct in place, she unconsciously sabotaged opportunities to seek new potential partners. She described how she would go with friends to a party in the hope of meeting someone but invariably decided there was never anyone who would like her. She would return home, deeply disappointed at another failure, as she saw it, but with her construct confirmed. She came to realize that she instinctively adopted a negative stance calculated to deter anyone who seemed to take an interest in her.

It was important for Olive to be able to recognize the thinking behind these acts of sabotage, which otherwise could have continued to strengthen this malevolent construct. Having taken the opportunity through counselling to review her previous experiences without prejudice, she was able to accept that her construct of there being "something wrong with her" was totally unfounded. Whilst it was unfortunate that things hadn't worked out to date, there was no reason to believe she was in some way unlovable, even if she was not immediately successful in finding someone with whom she could form a relationship.This gave her the courage to be more outgoing in her attitude.

If we find that one of our constructs is invalid, we have to replace it with something that anticipates the outcome of events more accurately. A child may believe firmly in Father Christmas—until she sees that the man in the santa outfit creeping into her room on Christmas Eve to hang a stocking at the end of her bed is her father. She is obliged, however reluctantly, to abandon the idea that there are magic figures in her life and this must probably include Rudolph, the tooth fairy, and the Easter bunny.

If, on the other hand, we refuse to accept the evidence that has invalidated our constructs, we can run into trouble. Rebecca, in her early thirties, came from a happy, energetic family, all the members of whom were self-employed. Her father was an architect, her brother a successful freelance journalist, and her sister had a thriving business in antiques restoration. Rebecca had always been interested in geneology and was good at digging up information to trace family lineages, which she did for several of her friends. She realized there was an opportunity here and, encouraged by her family, she started her own business.

For the first two years, she did very well, and was able to employ two assistants. However, with the development of on-line services which helped people trace their roots for themselves, she found her clients falling away until she was struggling to make ends meet. She came for counselling in a very anxious and depressed state, but, on the positive side, it soon became evident that her skills in research should enable her to find good employment in a number of areas. But Rebecca was not interested. Hers was a family in which the only mark of success was to be your own boss. The idea of reneging on this construct was, for her, simply unthinkable. She considered any discussion that might weaken her resolve to be downright dangerous, and rather than risk succumbing to temptation she abruptly discontinued therapy. It is saddening when this happens as there is always the thought that, given more time and opportunity to explore alternatives, a resolution might be achieved. Unfortunately, a construct that a person feels unable to abandon can lead to a kind of locked-in syndrome from which he cannot move.

As with all counselling, however practised, Kelly's construct is very much to do with interpretation—not just the problem as presented by the client, but why he is presenting it. Kelly felt very much as Carl Rogers did: the essence of counselling was to be able to step into the client's shoes.

Our constructs are somewhat like glasses through which we view the world and we look for evidence that can provide us with a convenient shorthand to confirm them. If you see a man driving a so-called sport utility vehicle in a major city, you may assume that this is simply his preferred form of transport. But if your tendency is to regard it as a "Chelsea tractor", you will probably think of it as brought in by the owner for no better reason than to create status for himself, and may resent the driver accordingly. In his writings, Kelly reminded counsellors always to keep an eye on their prejudices and to be cautious of first interpretations as they may reflect their own constructs at the expense of the therapeutic relationship.

We are often reluctant to admit to being biased, but it is essential that therapists are fully aware of their prejudicial constructs. This is one reason why counsellors in training are recommended to have counselling themselves. This might be interpreted as an instruction to follow the biblical edict "Physician, heal thyself". Some people have difficulty with this, questioning the need for therapy when they feel there's nothing wrong with them. This decree might be modified in psychotherapy to "Counsellor, know thyself". The purpose of working with an experienced psychotherapist, especially in the early days, is above all to facilitate the essential process of self-discovery.

* * *

We live in an age of increasing mobility but in many ways are tied to constructs that confine men and women to specific roles. The one-time German mantra "*Kinder, Küche, Kirche*", translated as "children, kitchen, church", and the English equivalent "Barefoot and Pregnant", reflect the idea that the woman's place is in the home, bearing children. Although these concepts might now be dismissed as derogatory, the fact remains that it is still difficult for women to achieve senior roles in government and business, although this may be slowly changing. The concept of the "house-husband" often produces depression in the man whose wife is the principal earner, however well the arrangement may be working, as he instinctively feels that his position runs counter to the basic construct of man as the breadwinner.

Environments, too, might be said to generate their own constructs. Any of us who have been to a hospital clinic will know that practically all patients, irrespective of their age, background, or authority in the outside world, assume a compliant and cooperative manner in this environment and will promptly obey the instructions of even the most junior nurse. To some extent, this implied authority can manifest itself in the counselling room, which is why creating an accepting and non-judgemental environment is an essential first step to ensuring that the client feels at ease.

In helping people discover themselves through analysis of their constructs, Kelly's approach has an affinity with another concept: Gestalt. *Gestalt*, a German word, can be broadly translated as the whole or complete configuration of something. The Gestalt school of psychology, established in the early part of the twentieth century, holds that individuals are more than simply the sum of their parts, and that drawing conclusions on the basis of one aspect of a person can be misleading. As such, Gestalt is described as a phenomenological-existential approach. (If you feel your eyes glazing over at this point, hold on: the concept is more accessible than it sounds.)

Phenomenology maintains that reality is not a fixed entity but consists of objects and events (phenomena) as they are perceived or understood in human consciousness. As with a person's constructs, the interpretations are considered as being unique to them. Existentialism reflects the fact that humans cannot escape the necessity of making sense of existence.

Gestalt therapy, which was introduced by Frederick (Fritz) Perls (1893–1970) and Laura Perls (1905–1990) in the 1940s, builds on this concept and emphasizes the importance in any psychological assessment of recognizing and working with every aspect of the individual—intellectual, physical, and emotional. Everything in the session is taken into account from the way that someone dresses and uses words, to the smallest nuances of body language and tone of voice.

As with Jung and Kelly, the central premise of Gestalt is that only if we fully understand ourselves are we in a position to make informed choices in life. Gestalt therapists focus on the immediate present, encouraging their clients to concentrate on their feelings, thoughts, and emotions as they experience them at that moment, and to stay with those feelings so they become aware of themselves in the fullest sense. If they feel their clients are holding back or not being wholly truthful with themselves, they may intervene, to overcome the barriers that may be obstructing progress. Thus, therapy may be quite an active process.

The point is that once we fully know ourselves we are in a much better position to assume responsibility for our decisions. As the sixteenth-century philosopher Francis Bacon (1561–1626) observed: Knowledge Is Power.

One of the devices Gestalt therapists deploy, as do those from other modalities, is the two-chair technique. This is designed to elicit the client's frustrations or resentments by inviting him to address an empty chair which is placed opposite to his own, and to imagine that it is occupied by a person to whom he wants to express his feelings. You have probably observed that often, when a person is talking to a friend about a run-in he has had with someone, he will enter into a dialogue in which he plays first himself, and then the other party involved. This helps to sustain interest and gives the account more authenticity. The listener hears not only the words that were exchanged, but also the way in which they were delivered, and may get some idea of the body language of the participants, the emotional environment, and perhaps something about the way the speaker sees him or herself.

So, someone might be heard saying to her companion: "And of course, he's there, glued to his computer as usual, and I go over and say to him (voice raised in anger and frustration) 'Do you think I'm a complete idiot?!' and he says (she drops her voice to an exaggerated, lazy drawl) 'No, but I think you do silly things sometimes.'" She now adopts the more neutral tone of a narrator. "Well, he has to realize that we can't go on like this. He has no respect for me. I'm fed up with being made to look as though I don't even know what day of the week it is."

Even from this short exchange we might conclude that the speaker perhaps tends to hear only what she wants to hear (he didn't agree she was an idiot), might resent activities that do not involve her, and may possibly be basing her sense of worth too much on the values accorded her by other people. From a counselling standpoint, material of this kind can be very revealing for the information it contains.

Sometimes the counsellor will have the client play the part of the difficult parent, unsympathetic partner, or awkward work colleague (whose dialogue and body language he can often reproduce to perfection) whilst the counsellor adopts the role of the client. By demonstrating a calmer, more reasoned response to the other party that he might take, the client may be brought to recognize the benefit of a different approach in which he does not allow himself to be so easily manipulated through his emotions.

Personal construct and Gestalt counsellors have to be good detectives in piecing together the nature and scale of their clients' life schemes and determining the true nature of their presenting problems. There is no on-screen record of George Kelly at work but he is an accessible writer. An understandable short book he wrote called *A Theory of Personality,* published in 1963, is still available if you would like to learn further from him at first hand.

You may recall in the previous chapter mention of the series of films entitled *Three Approaches to Psychotherapy* in which a client, Gloria, has half-hour sessions with three therapists, each working from a different orientation. Carl Rogers was the first, and the second was Fritz Perls. This session, too, can be seen on YouTube and provides an interesting glimpse of Gestalt therapy in action. At the start, Gloria is very shy and defensive but Perls is determined to bring out her true self as the only basis on which they can work. On the face of it, the meeting seems quite confrontational, but Perls works persistently to get Gloria to drop her guard and be the person she really is, which he eventually succeeds in doing. With a time-frame of only thirty minutes, the pace has to be somewhat forced, but the session serves as a reminder of how difficult it can be for us to move out of a protective environment we may have created for ourselves. If you see the video on YouTube you'll observe that Perls and Gloria smoke throughout the session—imagine such a situation today!

* * *

"And now," as Monty Python used to say, "for something completely different …"

CHAPTER SIX

Inter-relationships

O n the face of it, Eric Berne (1910–1970) might
not have been expected to bring about a significant new approach to psychotherapy. He had
wanted to practice psychoanalysis, and trained at the
San Francisco Psychoanalytic Institute. But when he
completed his course in 1956, he was loftily advised
that he was not yet ready for membership of the acad-
emy and should do further study before reapplying.
This was far from the disaster that it might have been,
as Eric Berne was spurred into pursuing his long-held
ambition to develop a completely new approach to
psychotherapy.

He was in accord with Freud that human nature is
comprised of interlinked components which affect our
behaviour and attitudes. Freud, you will recall, identified three such elements: the id, ego, and super-ego.
The id he saw as the basic animal in us; the ego, a part
of us that devises strategies to achieve the demands of
the id; and the super-ego, which represents our conscience and moral code.

But Berne wanted to move away from abstract analogies and metaphors. For him if a theory was to have true validity, it must be observable; that is, you had to be able to see it in action. Perhaps even more importantly, Berne wanted to make psychotherapy more accessible by using concepts and colloquial language that could be understood by everyone, professionals and clients alike. After years of development, he came up with a new approach to psychotherapy, which he called Transactional Analysis, or TA.

TA has four constituents. The first is a structural model that, like Freud's, incorporates three inter-connecting ego states, which Berne called Parent, Adult, and Child. These states reflect the way we think and act in any particular situation. We have all been children and, as children, have experienced the impact of parenthood and adult behaviour even before we were grown up. We therefore have the ability at any age to move into any one of these states, consciously or unconsciously. So, if we find ourselves on some occasions adopting a parent's attitudes and behaviour, we can be said to be in Parent ego state. A child who has been given charge of a younger sibling may well go into Parent mode, using her own experience of being parented as a template. Equally, a parent who finds herself thinking and feeling the way she did as a child will be in Child ego state.

The most straightforward of these ego states is the Adult. The Adult is regarded as the rational person within us who is straightforward, uses his or her resources productively and without prejudice, does not carry emotional baggage, and who is generally comfortable with themselves. This is an ideal state, and one to which we might aspire, but we can readily slip, perhaps inappropriately, into one of the other two.

Berne refined the categories of Parent and Child to reflect the different ways they could be within their ego states. He distinguished the Nurturing Parent (who could be father, or mother, or a carer), as someone who is concerned with keeping the Child safe and who offers unconditional love and support. The Controlling Parent, on the other hand, will focus on rules and discipline with the aim of helping the Child take his or her proper place in society. Soothing, supportive, bossy, or judgemental behaviour can all reflect aspects of Parent mode.

Berne saw the Child as having three states: the Natural Child, who is spontaneous and creative; the Rebellious Child, who tends to react against authority; and the Adaptive Child, who modifies his or her behaviour to accommodate the Parent, and who adjusts to the world as he or she experiences it.

Body language is also an indicator of an ego state. Angry or impatient gestures and expressions could signify Parent mode while rolling eyes, giggling, and sighing more closely fit with Child.

The second component of Transactional Analysis is the transactions themselves. A transaction is a unit of communication with another person. It can be verbal, but it doesn't have to be. A nod or an icy stare in response to a vocal initiative still counts as a transaction. Complementary transactions are said to occur when both people are in the same ego state, as between Parent and Parent, Adult and Adult, Child and Child, and Child and Parent. Crossed transactions are when the two parties are in conflicting ego states as in Parent–Adult or Adult–Child.

So, Geoff meets Jim on the way to the station. They exchange good mornings, and then Geoff goes on: "Did you see that party political broadcast? What a load of rubbish!" Jim replies: "Rubbish? Someone was finally talking sense!" Geoff says: "You can't really believe they'll keep their promises?" Jim rejoins: "They will, because they'll be in deep trouble if they don't!" And so on. Geoff and Jim may be questioning one another's political gullibility but they are both in Adult ego states and so these are complementary transactions. On this basis, they could go on indefinitely.

Take the following exchange:

He: I can't find my keys.
She: They're on the hall table.
He: Ah ... Right. Thanks.

Straight Adult to Adult. No problem. But crossed transactions often lead to trouble:

He: I can't find my keys.
She: (*heavy sigh*) Oh not again! You'd lose your head if it wasn't screwed on.
He: (*laughs*) I know!
She: (*slightly sourly*) They're on the hall table.

In response to his Adult statement, she has adopted Controlling Parent mode, hoping to force him into Child mode, and so demonstrate her superiority. But he isn't rising to it and stays in Adult ego state, obliging her to revert back to Adult state herself. But had he gone into C mode he may have responded: "You're always getting at me!" She could have then retorted: "Well, I need to, don't I?" This would possibly have kicked off a string of transactions likely to end in a row or sulks.

But equally, the man might have started in Child mode:

He: I can't find my keys! God, that's all I need!

She: Well, hold on. They can't be far.

He: If I miss my train ...!

She: Think a moment. What were you wearing yesterday?

He: Er—my—my blue suit.
(She goes to the wardrobe and fishes the keys out of his pocket.)

He: You've saved my life!

No conflict, because she has responded to his Child mode in Nurturing Parent mode—a complementary transaction. But note that it might have been quite convenient for him to start in Child ego state, knowing from experience that she would automatically adopt a Nurturing Parent role and do the work of finding his keys (or carrying out any other task) for him.

Complimentary exchanges, as in this Parent–Child example, are not necessarily productive:

Ben: *(aged thirteen)* Dad, can you give me a lift over to Shaun's place?

Dad: Why can't you cycle?

Ben: It's supposed to rain.

Dad: Well, wear your mac.

Ben: *(slightly whiney)* It'll be getting dark when I come back.

Dad: *(impatiently)* You've got lights on your bike, haven't you? What's the matter with you!

Here the Rebellious Child is up against the Controlling Parent. Theoretically complimentary though they may be, these exchanges have got Ben nowhere. But we can well see what's going on, and this fulfils Berne's requirement that a theory should be open to observation.

Anyway, tear up that script and try another approach:

Ben: Dad, could you give me a lift to Shaun's place, please?

Dad: Why can't you cycle?

Ben: I would, of course, but they say it's going to rain.

Dad: Well, you can wear your mac.

Ben: Oh, I know. It's just it'll be getting dark when I come back.

Dad: But, you've got lights ...

Ben: Yes, but I was just thinking—you've said yourself it's harder to see cyclists when the roads are wet and the wipers are going and there's dazzle from all the headlights ... (*He starts to turn away, adding in a small voice ...*) Well, I'll probably be OK.

Dad: No, I'd better take you.

This time Ben has started by playing the Adaptive Child, anticipating his father's rationale for cycling and avoiding confrontation. Dad's opening responses are less aggressive as a result. But Ben then slips over into Adult mode with a calm exposition on the potential impact of wet weather road conditions on cyclists, taking care to seem to be using his father's own words to add authenticity. So we are now witnessing a crossed transaction with Ben playing Adult while Dad is still in Parent mode. Adult–Parent transactions don't match. If Ben had stayed in Adult mode, he might have finished "... so I'll take extra care." This could have given time for his father to move into complimentary Adult mode himself, saying, perhaps, in adult language, "Yes, I think you're wise." But instead, Ben drops back into Child mode using words that automatically switch his, now slightly wrong-footed, father from Controlling into Nurturing Parent mode.

Now, in reality, Ben would have avoided any danger by cycling home along the footpath beside the road. But his father, in his chosen role of Controlling Parent, would frown on such anti-social behaviour, so he can hardly recommend it to his son, as Ben well knows. Dad's trapped and succumbs.

What Ben is doing here is playing a game. Game playing is the third major element of TA. One can think of a game as a series of interactions between two or more people leading to an outcome in which one individual or group obtains a payoff. Importantly, especially from a counselling standpoint, in many cases the participants of the games are unaware that there's a game going on, or if they are aware, they don't know how to fight their corner.

A common game is one that some couples can be seen to play on social occasions. They will talk amusingly about one another's perceived shortcomings with much pseudo-affection; but in fact are using the occasion as a perfect opportunity to air resentments and settle old scores, knowing that an outright row in public would be out of the question.

Some games are played so consistently that Berne reduced them to a shorthand of initials. IWFY, for example, stands for "If It Weren't For You", a scenario for which might be as follows.

Dave is married to Deborah. He has a somewhat mundane job working as a store manager. When he goes to the pub with his friends he talks wistfully of how he would love to do bungee jumping (or skydiving or windsurfing) but "my wife won't let me". Dave's message to her is "If it weren't for you, I'd be able to do these things". He is thus playing Child to her

Controlling Parent. But one day, Deborah says to him, "Oh, go on then. Why not?" She has moved to Adult state matching what she thinks is Dave's (thwarted) Adult. But Dave is aghast. The thought of bungee jumping actually terrifies him. His game is up. (It could be, on the other hand, that Deborah is on to him and is playing another well-known game, that of NIGY—Now I've Got You!)

But note that "If It Weren't For You" may be cruelly played by a parent on a child, especially a child that may not have been planned. "If it weren't for you, we could be holidaying in Greece …"; "If it weren't for you, we would be able to afford a new television …"; and so on. The child doesn't understand the "game" or how she is supposed to play it. She feels unwanted and unloved, often reduced to setting aside all her own needs and life choices in a desperate attempt to please the parent in every aspect of her behaviour—a strategy she can never win. This can have distressing long-term effects that quite often emerge in counselling.

Games are not limited to one exchange. They can go on for months, particularly if the other party is not aware of the game being played. In the days of National Service, which many young men resented for taking away two years of their lives, some recruits, especially in the early days, would adopt the ego state of Rebellious Child and play a game known as "drawing blankets", a phrase for professional skiving. The trick was to march purposefully around the barracks, eyes front, clutching a clipboard. When accosted by a "Controlling Parent" in the guise of a beady-eyed sergeant major, the recruit would return his look and state that he had been assigned to draw blankets or collect some piece of kit from the quartermaster's stores before marching off again. In this way, the experts among them managed to dodge all kinds of tedious group activities—drill parades, PT, and the like—by keeping a low profile. Actually, professional skiving was highly demanding. The perpetrator had to be on his guard, be neatly turned out, and show levels of initiative that would certainly have moved him up the ranks if applied differently. But for him, adhering to the motto "*nil carborundum*"—"Don't let 'em grind you down"—was reward enough.

One of the most enduring games is the Sulk. A classic example was the twenty-two year standoff between former prime ministers Ted Heath and Margaret Thatcher. Heath never forgave Thatcher for ousting him from the Tory leadership. Gordon Brown has been similarly accused of sulking because Tony Blair, in his view, for so long denied him his rightful turn at the helm of power.

Some couples stay together for years barely talking to one another because of a spat they may have had early on. Each has been determined that the other one should make the first consoling move or offer a worthwhile compensation for abandoning the sulk. This will never happen, as manipulating the sulk and creating games within it gives their lives a shared objective which they might otherwise not have had.

As you can see, the opportunities to play games with almost infinite variations are legion and they turn up regularly in counselling, the "loser" often being the one seeking therapy. In 1964, Berne published a book *Games People Play*, in which he analysed the whole psychological process of game playing. It was aimed at fellow therapists, but the public soon caught onto it and, to date, the book has sold more than five million copies. It is still in print.

In keeping with our quest for self-discovery, we need to be thoroughly aware of what games we ourselves may play. Do you know when you are playing games? And when you do, how successful are they? How often might you find yourself looking forward to a potential wrangle as providing an opportunity to try out your gamesmanship?

Counsellors can get caught up in their clients' games. The expectation is for an Adult–Adult relationship, but a client may, for example, have found that adopting a Child ego state has served them well, as it has often obliged others to adopt the matching ego state of Nurturing Parent. It is easy for counsellors in this situation to find they are adopting this same NP role themselves as a factor of transference. This can foster client dependence—exactly what the counsellor seeks to avoid.

The fourth component of TA is the Script, and the subject of a second book by Eric Berne called *What Do You Say After You Say Hello?* (1971) Berne held that from our earliest years we compose our life story, or script. As children, we build this script from the range of experiences we encounter and the parental programming we receive, adding detail and developing coping skills as we go along. In this, Berne's ideas relate closely to Kelly's personal construct approach.

Berne believed that once we have invested in a script, we take steps to ensure that it is not compromised because it seems to us to represent the best strategy for survival. We may therefore discount input that does not fit in with the scenario we have created. When we grow up we may not be aware of the continuing influence of earlier, perhaps simplistic, life scripts and how they may have led to an instinctive approach to life as adults. Using the metaphor of the fairy tale, Berne held that people may define themselves (or others) as winners or losers, princes or princesses—or frogs!

The concept of a life script and helping the client change aspects which are holding them back is, of course, the focus of all therapeutic approaches, whether through a process of self-discovery or active intervention by the therapist.

In terms of script structure, the most productive insight is one in which we see ourselves and the world as fundamentally healthy. Berne defined it as "I'm OK, You're OK". This is essentially an Adult–Adult mindset.

The person who takes the view "I'm OK, You're Not OK", is likely to be intolerant, and assume that others are against him or will not recognize his skills. He may see himself as a prince in a world of frogs, but may also hold a sneaky suspicion that the frogs are always on the lookout for opportunities to reduce his status. The concept "I'm OK, You're Not OK", can be seen as not just between "I" and "You", but a case of "Us" *vs.* the "Rest of the World". Thus, a member of a gang will take the view that he and his fellows are okay, but everyone else is not. This gives them a reason for banding together.

Someone, on the other hand, who has a low opinion of herself compared to others may adopt a "You're OK, I'm Not OK" approach to life. She believes she will be forever consigned to the role of frog, and may isolate herself or else exhaustively try to please the "princes" around her in the hope that they will give her the kiss that enables her to shed her amphibian skin. She will likely rebuke herself as always making the wrong decisions in life. Since she is determined she will never win, she may present as anxious and depressed.

Those that believe both they and their partners are Not OK, but that everyone else is OK, may sustain an enduring form of grievance.

The "I'm Not OK, You're Not OK" mind-set may well lead to severe psychosis.

However you may decide to practice, it can be valuable to recognize the different ego states in which clients may present themselves, their partners, and people at work. As described in the previous chapter, the two-chair technique is a useful tool, for this is where clients can reproduce not only the dialogue they exchange but each party's body language and tone of voice. If clients appear to be trapped in situations, even whilst recognizing that the situations are not healthy, it is often a reluctance to give up the "game" that leaves them stuck.

Have a look at the following three client presentations and see what Parent Adult Child events or variations of "OK-ness" may be taking place. These are all based on case history material, although, as elsewhere in this book, names and circumstances have been changed to preserve anonymity.

Hannah came for counselling obsessed by anger about what she perceived as her daughter's rank ingratitude. Hannah's childhood had been difficult: her father was often drunk and her mother short-tempered. From a very young age, she was often left in charge of her younger brother and had to devise a system of punishments and rewards within her limited means to keep him under control. She left home at seventeen and married a mild-mannered man twenty years her senior who reminded her of the father she wished she had had. They had two children, a son and a daughter. But they were at odds about how the children should be brought up, and Hannah felt she was "living a charade". The marriage ended in divorce.

Hannah got on well enough with her son but was closer to her daughter, Emily. She felt disappointed and obscurely let down when Emily left home at eighteen and married a man Hannah didn't approve of. For the sake of her grandchildren she stayed in touch, but the relationship was an uneasy one and Hannah found herself increasingly resenting Emily's husband. Then Emily's own marriage ran into difficulties and in a state of some distress she and her two small children came to live with Hannah. They managed well enough, but then Emily gradually recovered her independence, got a good job, and moved back to her own home. Hannah acknowledged that Emily had paid her way and had even bought her a new stove as a parting present, but she found herself becoming increasingly consumed with fury over what she perceived was her daughter's disloyalty. Why might this have been so?

* * *

When Martha's husband died, she was on her own and thankful that she had had two sons. Although they had both left home, they had all got on well as a family and the boys had initially been very supportive in the aftermath of their father's death. After that, life went on and Martha started to feel a little sorry for herself. Most of her friends were married couples and she felt somewhat isolated being without a partner. She felt her sons did not wholly appreciate her situation, and when they telephoned she would adopt a plaintive tone of voice and go on about how difficult life was for her now that their father was gone. Somewhat to her chagrin she found her sons began calling less often and if they came round seemed always to have an excuse for cutting their visits short. What might be happening here and what remedial action might Martha take?

* * *

Angus, twenty-three, came for counselling as he felt depressed. His father, who was retired from the army, had firm views about what was right and wrong, proper and improper. His mother broadly supported his father's views and Angus felt obliged to try to be the person they wanted. The family tended to isolate themselves from those they felt were not in accord with their opinions.

It was expected from the outset that Angus would join his father's regiment. He went to a school where there was a cadet corps but hated the army style of "pointless" discipline. He felt under pressure because his sister had trained as a doctor and his elder brother had joined the navy. Angus's real interest was in journalistic photography, but his father was hostile to this profession, having read about the "paparazzi" without really understanding the meaning of the term. Angus finally got a job with an estate agent and was sent round to photograph properties. As well as the standard views, he would take pictures from unusual angles to demonstrate his talent, but they were rarely used as the agents were concerned not to confuse potential buyers. Angus's relationships with women tended not to last as he would start by trying to please them but later demanded their unquestioning acceptance of everything he said or did. What could be happening here?

* * *

Looking back to Hannah, we can see that in being responsible for her younger brother, she was constantly obliged to adopt the role of Controlling Parent at an early age. This largely overshadowed her instinctive state of Natural Child. Even though she tried to escape into Adult mode by leaving home, her unfulfilled yearning for a loving father led her to marry a man who represented in part the benign or Nurturing Parent whose caring role she had not been able to experience. With the birth of her own children, she automatically dropped back into the Controlling Parent mode she had acquired in childhood. But her husband preferred the Nurturing Parent ego state that had originally attracted her. So although both parties were Parents they experienced many crossed transactions and the marriage broke up.

When Emily left home, Hannah was obliged to form an uneasy (from her standpoint) A–A relationship with her daughter and son-in-law. But when the marriage broke down, Emily was initially very dependent on her mother, much as she had been as a child. Her mother automatically resumed Controlling Parent state and her daughter that of Adaptive Child. This P–C relationship worked superficially for a short while, but as she recovered, Emily moved first to Rebellious Child and then to Adult. When Emily went back to her own home this was a major betrayal of an unspoken promise to maintain the P–C relationship, hence Hannah's fury. Fortunately, Hannah was able to understand what had happened and this helped her move towards a more self-accepting and liberating life script.

* * *

Martha's difficulty was resolved more easily. She realized she had been playing a game of being a Child in the hopes of persuading her sons to adopt the role of Nurturing Parents. Recognizing that they were disinclined to play along, she dropped her *faux* Child mode and returned to the Adult state she had previously shared with them. Her sons started to feel confident that they could visit her without encountering an agenda, and the relationship was restored.

* * *

We can look at Angus's situation from a standpoint of life positions. On the basis of the perceived successful career choices of his siblings, his script was probably "I'm not OK, You're OK". He fretted over the estate agent's rejection of his talents, so arbitrarily denying him OK-ness. On first acquaintance with women, he sought to achieve an "I'm OK, You're OK" relationship with them. However, he interpreted any criticism as reducing him to "frog" status, and relationships with the opposite sex broke up, with Angus adopting an "I'm Not OK, You're Not OK" stance.

The assessment of ego states and life positions is a matter of interpretation and does not in itself lead to a resolution of the client's problems. The TA counsellor will use this information as a foundation for therapy aimed at freeing clients of perceptions and beliefs that are preventing them from leading a fulfilled existence. Therapists from other orientations, whilst having the same objective of helping their clients, may not necessarily look for evidence of crossed ego states or games being played. But however the counsellor may practice, awareness of these factors in both themselves and their clients can make a valuable contribution to the therapeutic process.

* * *

It is evident from this, and the previous two chapters, that there is increasing commonality between different counselling approaches. Life scripts and constructs, and the beliefs we have about the world and our place in it, lead us to conduct ourselves and behave in particular ways. Very often our behaviour is automatic—a reflex reaction we may not always consciously initiate. In this situation we could be described as having been conditioned, insofar as a given stimulus will provoke an expected response. Recognition of this phenomenon led to the development of behaviourism, another approach to psychic management. Behaviourism can be highly effective, but it can also be used to achieve some startling and uncomfortable results, as we shall see.

CHAPTER SEVEN

The power of conditioning

Give me a child until he is seven, and I will give you the man.

> —Francis Xavier, co-founder of the Jesuit Order
> (attributed)

The quotation above reflects the potential influence of conditioning. It suggests that if children are brought up from the earliest years to respond in a particular way to certain stimuli in the form of events or situations, these responses will be locked into their minds and cannot be changed. This brings us to the question: How well might we recognize the influence of childhood conditioning? And, importantly, if this conditioning is proving unproductive for us or our clients, how might it be changed or modified?

The most straightforward example of stimulus/response behaviour is that which, if not completely out of our control, is largely automatic. A tickle in the throat produces the reflex action of a cough. We yawn when we are tired (or bored!), and instinctively change position if we are uncomfortable. We're hardly aware of the processes and coughs or sneezes are quite difficult to suppress unless we catch them very early. These are defined as innate responses.

Next comes the behaviour that is learned in response to a positive or negative event. You will almost certainly have heard of "Pavlov's dogs". Ivan Pavlov (1849–1936) was a Russian physiologist who, early in the nineteenth century, was using dogs to study the relationship between salivation and digestion. For this, he set up a system to collect the animals' saliva which automatically flowed the moment they started to eat—a standard innate response. But then he found that as the animals became familiar with the routine, they would start to salivate just at the sight of him. He was intrigued by this, and erected screens around their cages so they couldn't see when he was coming. Taking the experiment a step further, he would produce a range of different sounds—whistles, bells, music—some of which he would make just before he delivered the food through to them. He found that in each case the dogs would learn to associate a particular sound with food, and would drool accordingly. This is the classic example of the conditioned reflex. Importantly, Pavlov also noted that the dogs would salivate when they heard an associated sound, irrespective of whether food was produced or not.

Pavlov's experiments were built upon by an American psychologist, John B. Watson (1878–1958), who had also worked with animals. Watson held the radical view that in terms of classical conditioning, human beings were essentially no different from other creatures.

His doctrine, which he called "behaviourism", is that human psychology is the product of our experiences in life, our upbringing, education, and environment. The behaviourist takes the view that we are all born alike with no preconceptions, complexes, or intrinsic likes or dislikes. Our minds are essentially a clean slate. We become what we are through the process of conditioning.

It can be imagined that a toddler straying into a field past a "Beware of the Bull" notice would fearlessly wander towards its occupant, having no reason to assume she was in danger. She would only learn to be alarmed when her appalled parents rush in to retrieve her. Watson actually carried out an experiment in which he placed a nine-month-old baby boy (known as "Little Albert") in a room. He introduced him in turn to a large dog, then a monkey, and finally a rat. Albert reacted with natural curiosity, but without fear, to all of them. Later in the experiment when Watson brought on the rat, an assistant positioned behind Albert would beat a loud, discordant gong which the boy found very distressing. Every time the rat was brought in, the gong was sounded.

Eventually, poor Albert was reduced to tears just at the sight of not only the rat, but of any similar type of animal. (Had the arrival of the rat been accompanied by a pleasant tune, Albert might have developed a deep affection for furry creatures.) So, by this token, emotions are learned, not inherited. Watson called the process of repeatedly inducing a behavioural pattern in response to a given stimulus "positive reinforcement". Behaviour that is consistently rewarded by an unpleasant event being avoided he called "negative reinforcement". The child who obediently settles down to do her homework after tea may do so to avoid the less pleasant alternative of having to help with the washing up.

In defence of his approach to psychology, Watson famously wrote:

> Give me a dozen healthy infants, well-formed, and my own specified world to bring them up in and I'll guarantee to take any one at random and train him to become any type of specialist I might select; doctor, lawyer, artist, regardless of his [sic] talents, penchants, tendencies, abilities, vocations and race of his ancestors.[1]

He added: "I am going beyond my facts, and I admit it, but so have the advocates of the contrary." Watson's last observation neatly points to the defensive attitude adopted by many pioneers of psychology.

As the quotation at the beginning of the chapter shows, Watson was not alone in his thinking. In an army, for example, "square-bashing", the wearing of uniforms, authoritarian routines, ritualized respect for rank, and adherence to strict dogma all condition the soldier to obey unthinkingly commands which, in a life-threatening situation, he might otherwise hesitate to comply with. New entrants to schools, particularly boarding schools, are immediately inducted into "school traditions" so that they conform to a hierarchal structure. Attitudes and ways of thinking often persist into later years long after the conditioning process has passed into the unconscious. In the counselling environment, if the impact of conditioning is not recognized, the client may present a confusing or contradictory picture.

A classic example of individual conditioning features is in Anthony Burgess' 1962 novel *A Clockwork*

Orange in which the protagonist, Alex, is injected with a substance that induces severe nausea, while being forced to watch filmed scenes of violence, the aim being to condition him to avoid committing violent acts himself. As an extra twist, Alex is coincidentally forced to hate the music of Beethoven which is played on the soundtrack of the film.

Watson's definition of the conditioned reflex paved the way for the next behavioural researcher, Edward ("Ted") Thorndike (1874–1949). Thorndike placed a cat in a cage which he called "a puzzle box". The cat could escape only by moving a lever and operating a latch. The poor old moggy at first floundered around, but eventually would accidentally trigger the steps that opened the door, so enabling it to reach a plate of food. Through a process of trial and error the cat became increasingly proficient at the task, so it could escape without delay. Thorndike called this "the law of effect", which states that once a rewarding form of behaviour is learned, it remains rooted in the mind.

Building on Thorndike's work comes B. F. Skinner (1904–1990). Skinner introduced a further dimension to "behaviourism"—operant conditioning. "Operant conditioning" is a simple feedback system. If, when we do something, we are rewarded for it, then we're more likely to repeat what we've done. Equally, if an action is followed by punishment the reverse occurs. Thus, future behaviour is determined by the consequences of past events. On the basis of this thesis, Skinner claimed that the mind and consciousness were irrelevant and that psychology should focus only on measurable behaviours. He conducted numerous experiments to demonstrate that operant conditioning is a powerful learning tool. In one of these he put a pigeon in a cage. Above the feeding bowl was a small aperture behind which was a disk that could be rotated to display different words. If the bird pecked at the disk when the word "peck" was displayed it would release a catch which lifted its seed tray into the cage. Pecking the disk when other words were displayed produced no result.

Through trial and error the pigeon learned to peck the disk when it read "peck" and to ignore other words. It had not, of course, learned to read. The word would have elicited no response outside that particular environment. To note is that Skinner did not always reward the first correct peck, in which case the pigeon would stab at the notice harder and more persistently before finally giving up.

The effects of trying to break a cycle of conditioning can often be observed where a client's decision to stop responding to other people's demands meets with fierce opposition from those other people.

An example of this was Maria, who came for counselling because she felt that some people were "trespassing on her good nature". She referred in particular to a neighbour for whom she had done a number of favours, but who seemed to take for granted that she would always be available on demand and barely bothered to thank her. Maria pronounced herself as being on the whole happy and self-assured as she had lots of friends, but realized that she sometimes put her own interests "on the back burner" and wanted guidance on how to get "my boundaries right".

Maria was helped to be more self-accepting and less dependent on other people's goodwill, politely declining to undertake tasks which she felt would be unrewarding. As often happens, she found this much harder than she had anticipated. Her neighbour, and others whom she had previously obliged, resented these changes and in various ways applied emotional pressure on her to continue to be the person who would go to the shops for them or do free babysitting—in effect, jabbing at the "peck" plate. But Maria kept her nerve, and eventually her fair-weather friends melted away and she was able to identify and relate healthily to people who truly cared about her.

In 1951, a further major experiment in human behaviour was conducted by Solomon Asch (1907–1996), a Polish-born American psychologist. He was interested in the conflict between the instinct to act in accordance with one's senses and the desire to conform to the views of others. He conducted a now classical experiment in which a group of students were invited to match a vertical line drawn on the left-hand side of a board with one of three lines of slightly differing lengths displayed on the right. It was immediately clear to the unbiased viewer which were the matching pair.

One of the group in Asch's study was a genuine student. What this student didn't know was that the other "students" were actors—"stooges", as they're known in the trade. When asked which two lines matched, all the other "students" gave the wrong answer. At first the real student followed his senses, and although puzzled by his colleagues' responses, gave the right answer. The exercise was repeated several times with different variations and every time the stooges made a mismatch. Eventually, the real student's desire to conform became so powerful it overwhelmed his reason and he gave the wrong answer along with all the others. This experiment reflects the fact that humans are social creatures who feel a strong need to be in accord with those around them.

This phenomenon can sometimes be seen with young people, who may find themselves as part of a group whose ideas and behaviour are basically in conflict with their own. They may not be fully aware of this and become anxious without understanding why. In the unprejudiced and accepting environment of the counselling room, such clients may return to the script they devised for themselves in childhood, only to find themselves reverting to the group ethics when in the company of the pack.

In 1961, at the time when Adolf Eichmann was standing trial in Israel for his role in organizing the Holocaust, an assistant professor of psychology at Yale University, Stanley Milgram (1933–1984), puzzled over how it was that members of the Schutzstaffel (SS) came to treat those in the concentration camps with such appalling inhumanity. He did not believe that they could be intrinsically different to anyone else, and to test his theory invited members of the public to participate in what he called "a research project on learning and memory".

Volunteers of both sexes and of varying ages and backgrounds assembled in a room and were given a few minutes to get to know one another. In charge of the operation was a man in a white coat, who introduced himself as a professor and who explained the procedure to follow in a calm, measured way. The participants were split into "teachers" and "learners", by drawing lots. The teachers watched as the learners were strapped into wired chairs, through which they could be administered electric shocks. The teachers were then led to another room and seated in front of a panel with a line of switches through which they could administer progressively severe discharges to the learners. The switch at the far end of the board would send out a current of 450 volts—quite enough to kill. A television relay enabled the teachers to see and hear what was going on in the next room. At the start, the teachers were told to give the learners a 50 volt test shock—sufficient to make the learners jump and to assure the teachers of the authenticity of the programme.

The learners were then given pairs of words which they were expected to memorize so that if one word of a pair was later repeated, they should be able to select the correct companion word. The testing began, and every time a learner gave a wrong answer, the teachers were instructed to give them a progressively more powerful shock. As the voltage increased, the learners began to yell in pain or even seemed to be suffering heart attacks. At various stages, each of the teachers wanted to stop, but the professor seemed quite unmoved and told them that they must continue in the interests of research. He emphasized they had no option. The question was: Would the teachers ultimately refuse to carry on, or would they accede to the authority of the professor? Of the forty participants in the study, twenty-six delivered the maximum shocks; only fourteen stopped before this point.

As you will have guessed, all the "learners" were stooges and no electric shocks were actually administered, but great care was taken to ensure that the true volunteers, the "teachers", could not know this, although they were debriefed after the sessions.

So why did so many of the participants in this experiment behave in such a seemingly sadistic way? The answer would seem to be that we have inbuilt conditioning that makes us obey someone we perceive as a competent authority—whether scientist, mesmerizer, or dictator—and to set aside moral judgements when being instructed by such an authority. As might be expected, the experiment caused much harrumphing about ethics and it seemed unlikely it would ever be repeated.

But astonishingly, a show on French television in 2010 entitled *Le Jeu de la Mort* (*The Game of Death*) produced exactly the same results. A (stooge) "learner" was invited to sit in an electrically wired chair in a compartment on stage. Volunteers from the audience were asked in turn to come up and sit in front of a control panel. When the stooge gave wrong answers to questions from the show's compère, the volunteer, if instructed by the audience to do so, would administer increasingly severe electric shocks to the "learner". Members of the audience were given every reason to believe that the shocks being inflicted on the stooge were real and that they caused excruciating pain. But such is the authority even of television that the audience (led on by more stooges strategically placed amongst them) invariably voted for punishment. On their instruction, 80% of the volunteers, despite stating their misgivings, administered apparently lethal shocks to their victims—an even higher number than in Milgram's original experiment.

Other less intrusive, but equally informative, experiments have shown how we may unthinkingly behave in accordance with preconceived criteria in everyday life. Using the techniques of Candid Camera, it was shown that if a group of people waiting for a green light for clearance to cross a road saw a confident-looking, well-dressed individual ignoring the signal and crossing the street anyway, they would follow on. But if someone dressed in T-shirt and patched jeans crossed over when the light was red, they would stay put.

These demonstrations serve to remind us not only of our clients' susceptibility to conditioning, but also our own. This is not to suggest that we are all sheep at heart. Such experiments work only in highly ordered environments. We need only to look at the long history of human endeavour from the conquering of Everest to the 2,000 people who have been awarded the George Medal for "extreme acts of bravery, courage, or gallantry in the face of danger" to confirm our independence.

Behaviour therapy, as you might expect, focuses on eradicating unhelpful conditioning by helping the client to adopt productive alternatives with the help of a range of strategies. It is essentially a practical approach, since the therapist is primarily concerned with finding the means of altering maladaptive behaviour and its immediate causes. Where conditioning is firmly in place, it can be hard and even unpleasant for the client to make the desired moves, so the therapist looks for ways of rewarding changes in behaviour.

Simon came for counselling because he felt extremely anxious whenever he had to drive anywhere. Just getting behind the wheel started a feeling of panic. This greatly restricted his freedom of movement. He was not a nervous driver as such. He used to have a motorbike and once even did some training on a skid pan, which he greatly enjoyed.

His history revealed that some fifteen years earlier, when driving to work one day, his heart had seemed to flutter and then slow down. He became dizzy and feared he would lose consciousness. He managed to pull over to the side of the road and after a few moments, his symptoms subsided. Simon realized he had been very concerned that a colleague at work seemed likely to be promoted over him and had decided he must speak to his manager about it, which he knew he would find difficult.

His doctor suggested he had simply had a panic attack because of his state of mind at the time.

But then Simon experienced further episodes of his heart behaving oddly, often at times when he was not worrying about anything. He became progressively more fearful of driving in case he should suddenly lose control and have an accident. Finally, he consulted a cardiologist who determined that the erratic behaviour of his heart was due to a block in the conduction system which could be corrected by inserting a pacemaker, and this was duly carried out.

But by now, Simon had been so conditioned into associating driving with extremely unpleasant feelings that even though he knew the problem with his heart had been resolved, it made no difference. He was unable to distinguish the reality from the fantasy and experienced the same feelings if he simply visualized himself driving.

Several behavioural ploys were initiated to help him, in a process called "systematic desensitization". First, he undertook to drive short distances with an experienced instructor in the passenger seat, assured in the knowledge that the instructor would know how to deal with sudden loss of control. With his confidence a little restored, he then drove with a friend, also a driver, by his side, and finally with someone who had not yet learned to drive. Following the principles of positive reinforcement, Simon was encouraged always to choose a destination that offered the prospect of a reward, rather than going on a journey to perform a task. He enjoyed visiting historic sites and going for country walks, so trips were planned accordingly.

Even then, he found the going tough and had to fight his desire to turn back before the target was achieved. As supportive therapy he was encouraged to adopt simple relaxation techniques, and he attended yoga classes to help with this.

Long distance driving was still his hardest task. He had a young son and was asked: "Supposing you learned that your son had been kidnapped and the terms of his release was that you must drive 200 miles on your own to rescue him, would you go?" Simon acknowledged that of course he would, without hesitation. From a behavioural therapy standpoint this would be the equivalent of "flooding", a technique in which a subject is exposed to the most extreme anxiety-provoking situation in one go. The argument is that if Simon had coped with being behind the wheel on his own for two to three hours, driving off to work the following day would be small beer by comparison.

Another technique, behaviour modification, includes habit-reversal training, such as painting fingernails with a bitter substance so as to stop people biting their nails, which they often do unthinkingly. The drug Antabuse® (disulfiram) produces an extremely unpleasant effect if even a small amount of alcohol is consumed. These approaches require active participation from the client at the outset.

Sometimes, however, the motivation for change can be so powerful that it can extinguish unproductive behaviour at a stroke.

Denis wanted help in controlling his anger and dealing with his sense of low self-worth. He was extremely sensitive to criticism and if he made even a small mistake at work would agonize about it all day. His attention would sometimes wander from the task in hand, and he had been fired from a previous job on account of this. Although not an alcoholic, Denis acknowledged that he and his wife were quite heavy drinkers.

The couple often had unedifying rows and he revealed that ten days earlier one of their quarrels, when both were drunk, had escalated into extreme violence. They were in the kitchen. He had grabbed a knife and she a heavy carving fork and they had gone for one another. In the ensuing struggle he had cut her just below the neck and she had stabbed him in the arm. Although neither wound was serious, both were shocked by the realization that it could have ended very differently. They determined that this time they would really stay clear of alcohol.

At the start of counselling, Denis was quite depressed by his behaviour and guilty over his lack of self-control. He and his wife had agreed to give up drinking on previous occasions, but within days they had fallen back into their old ways. But, rather to his surprise, this time their resolve seemed to be holding out. They had continued to abstain from alcohol and in the following weeks, matters began to take a turn for the better. Denis found his self-confidence increasing, he felt more clear-headed, and was starting to enjoy his work. His relationship with his wife became much warmer, and from just getting by financially, they suddenly had an extra £100 a week in their pockets—the amount they would have spent previously on drink. Denis even got promoted at work. So the rewards for their abstention were clearly evident. Such progress may be gratifying for the counsellor, but the most influential factor for Denis was the realization that this time they might really have been able to break their habit. Life wasn't perfect, and he and his wife would sometimes quarrel, but they were expecting their first child and were looking to move out of rented accommodation and pay a mortgage.

Of course, in such situations there is no certainty that everything will continue to go smoothly, and the counsellor still has an important role in providing support and encouragement to help the client to stay on track and deal with setbacks.

Behaviour therapy may also be effective in providing parents with a structure to manage children with attention deficit disorders (ADDs) through rewarding positive behaviour. Sufferers of obsessive compulsive disorder, or OCD, can be helped through a progressive programme of clear, small steps, to manage their anxiety and control their impulses for repetitive behaviour. As with all behavioural approaches, the counsellor gives positive reinforcement through encouragement, helping clients to keep to the forefront of their mind the rewards of achievement. They may also be asked to keep a record of their progress so they do not condemn themselves if they have the occasional relapse.

Phobias, defined as irrational persistent fear of certain situations or things, are also amenable to behaviour therapy. There are literally hundreds that have been identified, from ablutophobia, a fear of bathing or washing, to zemmiphobia, a fear of the great mole rat! With agoraphobia, for example, which is the fear of being in crowded places, a behavioural therapist may agree a treatment plan based on a series of practical steps to enable clients to achieve the goal of managing to function in such an environment.

But in parallel with this practical approach, the counsellor will likely work with the client to explore the thoughts and beliefs that may have given rise to their fears or anxiety in the first place and which may be sustaining their behaviour. Rather than focusing just on what the person does, there are clear benefits for understanding why she is doing it, and what messages she is giving herself.

Returning to Simon for a moment. He was helped to recognize that it was the fear of a panic attack and its attendant discomfort when driving that was controlling him, rather than being in danger from a cardiac malfunction that had, in any event, been corrected. He also came to accept that whilst a bout of acute anxiety was very unpleasant, it was not life-threatening, and he could certainly tolerate it. Counselling that seeks to help through drawing on our perceptions and powers of reasoning is called "cognitive therapy", and in many ways is a natural companion to the behavioural approach. This has given birth to two combination therapies: Cognitive Behaviour Therapy, or CBT, and Rational Emotive Behaviour Therapy, or REBT.

An exploration of these approaches is the subject of the next chapter.

Note

1. Watson, J. B. (1930). *Behaviourism* (revised edn). University of Chicago Press.

CHAPTER EIGHT

Automatic thoughts and irrational beliefs

It's not what happens to you; but how you react to it that matters.

—Epictetus, philosopher, AD 55–136

When you think about it, this declaration by the Stoic philosopher, Epictetus, is extraordinarily powerful. It implies that no one but ourselves has authority over how we should think or feel. And with that authority comes the empowerment to decide how we will respond to any given situation, positive or negative. It is this capacity within us that was recognized by the initiators of a new approach to counselling—the cognitive therapies.

As already discussed, George Kelly held that we build constructs from our earliest childhood. These constructs influence our thoughts, beliefs, and behaviour. Kelly also recognized that this is an active process, in that we continually adjust our thinking according to experience, so as to enable us to anticipate events and respond to them productively. He saw us as scientists, using practical data to arrive at a consensus of how best to lead our lives. We have to make judgements and act on them, for, if we didn't, we would never learn. But whether our learning is always productive is another matter.

Cognitive psychology is founded on the idea that these constructs sometimes lead us to flawed processing of information, bringing in its wake irrational or defective concepts about ourselves, others, or life in general. We may not always realize this is happening, so do not always take the corrective measures to change the thinking and behaviour that are perpetuating a situation. As a consequence, we experience emotional difficulties and fall back into self-defeating responses. Freud and Jung believed our emotional problems were the outcome of concealed forces in the unconscious over which we have no control. Everything needed interpretation by the psychoanalyst or psychiatrist. But cognitive psychology recognizes that whilst we may sometimes get things wrong, we have within us the tools to make corrections if our way of dealing with events or situations is shown to be ineffectual. Our thinking has been learned, but what has been learned can be unlearned.

Although there are a number of present-day practitioners working with variations of cognitive therapy, the founding fathers are generally recognized as Aaron T. ("Tim") Beck (1921–) and Albert Ellis (1913–2007). Both men practised in the 1950s and both were psychoanalysts for several years before they became disenchanted with what they perceived were the limitations of this approach and started adopting cognitive techniques with their patients. They worked in slightly different ways reflecting their individual temperaments. But they respected one another's work.

We'll start with Beck. As with other practitioners of psychoanalysis, Beck found that there were anomalies in what his patients presented. Although they might seem to be openly talking about events in their lives, he would detect elements of emotion or behaviour that didn't quite fit their presentations. Beck took the view that this was because they weren't fully aware of the process that led them to respond to some situations the way they did, and he developed the concept of "automatic thoughts". Automatic thoughts can be defined as shortcuts between an event and our response to it. If we go to pick up a saucepan from the stove and find that the handle has become very hot, we'll quickly let it go. We don't consciously say to ourselves "It would be inadvisable to remain attached to this object, as the heat from it may damage my hand", although this is, of course, the thought that drives our action.

Such automatic thoughts are easy to identify, but if we don't recognize them they may warp our emotions and lead to unproductive behaviour.

Irene comes for counselling because she has recently been experiencing bouts of anxiety that seem to come from nowhere. She is in her late seventies. She leads an active life, enjoying walking and the company of friends. But recently she has become listless, spending long hours in bed. Some six months earlier she learned that a contemporary from her schooldays, whom she recalled as being particularly lively and adventurous, had died. She is sad about this, but can see no reason for feeling anxious.

When this is explored in session, she comes to realize that the event had reminded her of her own mortality, her automatic thought being "I'm the same age as she was—I suppose I'll be next". Her recognition of this thinking enables her to put matters into perspective. Yes, it could happen to her, and one day she will die, but there was no reason why a friend's departure should herald the end of her own life.

Our interpretation of any experience is based on a hypothesis, a theory, about what is going on and what, if anything, this says about us. This theory will be based on how we have constructed our own views of what is right or wrong, safe or dangerous. A single event may also lead to a whole series of hypotheses, each with its own emotional and behavioural consequences.

Jack works as a junior manager in a manufacturing company. His good morning greeting to his boss is usually returned, but the past couple of days the man has ignored him, walking straight past Jack's desk and into his office, shutting the door firmly behind him. Outwardly, Jack shrugs it off. If his boss is in a sour mood, that's his problem. But then he finds himself starting to get angry. He tells himself that it must be because he resents being treated with disrespect. But behind this lies an unspoken corollary—if his boss isn't polite to him it's because he doesn't have to be; Jack simply isn't worth the effort.

So Jack's anger is soon superseded by unfocused feelings of anxiety. His unconscious processing here is that if he's not worth anything, why bother to keep him on? His wife is shortly expecting another child and this is no time to be out of a job. Jack now subliminally recalls other instances where he felt undervalued and he starts to feel depressed.

None of these emotional states will serve him well as they can evoke behaviour which is unlikely to be beneficial to him. Having told himself that his input is not valued, Jack may adopt a surly attitude to express the injustice he feels. He perhaps starts to make derogatory comments about his boss and moan about the way the company is run. If his work colleagues become fed up with this and start to avoid him, it proves to Jack the word's got around that he might be for the chop. As a protective measure, he may try to stay clear of his boss to avoid further evidence of rejection. Such maladaptive thinking can easily become a habit, so that Jack anticipates rejection outside the work environment as well. This can then impact on his social and family relationships. He may adopt a superior, hostile attitude when meeting new people to protect his self-esteem.

Beck was very much aware of how thoughts can influence emotions. When he was an intern he started to feel unwell and became depressed. He recalls his mind was full of negative thoughts: his job couldn't last; his relationship with his wife was deteriorating. He even thought of leaving medicine. It was only when a colleague asked if he had noticed how yellow he was that the reality emerged. He had hepatitis, a disorder that could be treated. His depression went and with it his negative thoughts about his work and his marriage. But he felt his depressed feelings, although based on a false premise, could be understood in light of his state of mind at the time. So other people might make similar assessments of themselves that were flawed but which reflected their disposition in the circumstances in which they found themselves.

Beck took the line that we can only work on what we understand. If we don't know why we're responding to an event in a particular way we're hardly in a position to correct any maladaptive thinking. Cognitive counselling is about processing information. The goal is not simply to identify and correct a person's faulty evaluations, but by working with them to test their suppositions, help them acquire the skills of evaluating their beliefs and behaviour. Once our thoughts are revealed to us, we can start to question the logic of our ideas, and, in the light of our knowledge, develop coping strategies which enable us effectively to become our own counsellors.

Going back to Jack's situation: a cognitive therapist would explore with him what evidence there is that his employer's lack of response means that he is dissatisfied with Jack's work or has no respect for him. Could it be that he was simply preoccupied? Had anyone else noticed changes in his general attitude? Jack may then recall that a couple of major orders had recently been cancelled and that this could well have created cash-flow problems—enough to preoccupy any company director. From this, he may acknowledge that his thinking had been too narrowly focused and had not taken sufficient account of other factors. He also reflects that he has, after all, done quite well in his job and been promoted since he joined. And whilst there are some people he doesn't get on with, there are others whom he knows value his opinion. With this more realistic assessment of his situation, his emotional state improves.

The cognitive therapist will not simply point out possible flaws in a client's thinking and how he might contest them; she will encourage the client to work out the solutions for himself through a process described as "guided discovery". As a part of this approach, the therapist will use a form of enquiry called "Socratic questioning". Socrates (469–399 BC), the classical Greek philosopher, taught his students by asking questions designed to help them think the answers through

themselves. So, investigations such as "What do
I tell yourself when this happens?", "How do you
think behaving in this way may help?", "What sort
of advice would you give a friend in this situation?",
and "What would need to happen for things to be better?" will encourage the client to think through their
responses and test their logic. It is far more productive
for us to amend our own constructs rather than have
someone else tell us what we should be doing. This
somewhat equates to the proverb "Give a man a fish
and feed him for a day; teach him to fish and feed him
for a lifetime".

Beck talked of "learning to learn" as an important
part of our successfully making changes. A feature of
the cognitive approach is the use of homework. In session, a client may agree that her thinking is flawed, but
away from the counselling room her long-established
automatic thoughts may cut in, so she may well find
herself responding to a situation just as she has always
done. To combat this, she will be encouraged to keep a
written record of when she finds herself becoming anxious or experiencing feelings of guilt, and what thoughts
are going through her mind to create these moods. The
next step is for her to challenge these thoughts, and
if she recognizes that they are illogical, to focus on
alternative ways of thinking that are realistic and supported by evidence. If her mood lightens, it is likely
that her alternative thinking is more consistent with
reality. In this way, she practises the skills of adopting a more productive mindset, which should gradually
replace the biased automatic thoughts that have been
holding her back.

Homework assignments may involve experimenting
with new ways of behaving. Returning finally to Jack,
his counsellor might encourage him to adopt a more

outgoing attitude, continuing to greet his boss as he has always done. With the recognition that his worth is not dependent on other people's inferred opinions, Jack can afford a more positive attitude towards his colleagues. What may start as a cautious experiment in play-acting may soon acquire an authority of its own.

Cognitive therapy, which Beck later modified to cognitive behavioural therapy, reflects the inter-relationship between what we think and what we do. It is essentially a collaborative enterprise, a joint effort between client and counsellor. As with Rogers, the therapeutic relationship is based on genuineness, empathy and unconditional positive regard. The counsellor respects the client's viewpoint and the basis on which she has adopted it.

Automatic thoughts can be difficult to deal with precisely because they are often so elusive. Counsellors have to be aware of assigning obvious causes for emotional states and be able to adopt a structure from which they can analyse feelings and behaviour that may seem to be at odds with a given situation. A workbook, *Mind Over Mood: Change How You Feel by Changing the Way You Think* (1995), by two leading American clinical psychologists, Dennis Greenberger and Christine Padesky, provides a very practical approach for undertaking such exercises.

* * *

Like Beck, Albert Ellis had also become disenchanted with psychoanalysis, finding that his clients still remained bogged down with unproductive thinking and behaviour after many sessions. But whereas Beck held that emotional disorders arise through distortions of reality, Ellis took the view that we are biologically programmed to think irrationally.

For example, we are disposed to trust the judgement of "celebrities" of whatever stamp, which is why they are so often used to endorse products in advertising about which they may actually know little or nothing. We tend to seek evidence that supports the views we hold and the decisions we have made and ignore that which does not fit in. We readily stereotype people from the flimsiest information if they seem to fall into categories with which we are familiar. We may buy two for the price of one regardless of need, simply because we must go for a bargain.

It is reasonable to want to be liked and approved of, to wish to succeed in our endeavours, to anticipate that our good deeds will be acknowledged, and to hope that others will meet our moral criteria. But Ellis believed our irrational tendencies may result in our hoisting these preferences into dogmatic, unrealistic demands: we *must* be approved of or there is something wrong with us; we *must* succeed in all that we do or we are worthless; and life *must* be comfortable, for it would be intolerable if it were not.

Like so many before him, Ellis's approach to therapy was significantly influenced by events in his early years. He had a difficult childhood. An operation to remove his tonsils when he was four went wrong and he nearly died from blood poisoning. Over the next three years he was frequently consigned to hospital with malfunctioning kidneys, sometimes for extended periods and with only infrequent visits by his parents. Ellis developed a concern for his health and never engaged in the rough-and-tumble games of normal boyhood. Not surprisingly, he grew up painfully shy. At school he avoided social situations where possible and was terrified if he was required to stand up in class and recite a poem or put in any other way under the spotlight. In his solitude, he turned to reading across a broad spectrum and became intrigued by the concepts of philosophy.

He came to realize that he would not get far in life unless he made some radical changes to his thinking and behaviour. Here his interest in philosophy served him well. He took the advice of Epictetus and determined that he would free himself of disabling emotions and behaviour by proving he could take on extreme discomfort and survive. For example, he dealt brutally with his shyness by forcing himself to chat to girls he would accost in the local park. When he was rebuffed, he would remind himself that it was his overtures that were being rejected, not him. With this belief held firmly in place, he was able to largely free himself from social anxiety by accepting himself for the person he was.

He called his approach to counselling Rational Therapy, but later modified this to Rational Emotive Therapy in acknowledgement of the close link between reason and feelings. In accordance with behavioural therapy, he realized that conditioning played a major role in how people responded to life events and that people could overcome their problems through action as well as insight. With this in mind, in 1993 he changed the name again to Rational Emotive Behaviour Therapy.

Jenny is a member of a theatre company which puts on plays at the local community hall. She is a well-respected performer, but in their latest production she has turned her hand to directing. However, she becomes very anxious as the opening night gets closer. Although rehearsals seemed to be going fairly well, she is increasingly unsure that she is up to the task. After the first performance she feels the applause is rather muted, and that this must be a reflection of her poor directing skills. Jenny sees this as signifying that she's a failure and she becomes depressed. Moreover, thinking herself a failure, she starts to behave with lessened confidence in other situations.

A CBT therapist will explore her thinking and question the evidence that she is unsuccessful as an artistic director, but the REBT therapist will also have her consider the possibility that she might not be as good a director as she would wish. This may seem harsh, but if Jenny had told herself that such a conclusion would be too awful to contemplate, as it would confirm she was a failure, she would put herself into a no-win situation. By factoring in and facing up to a worst-case scenario, Jenny will be in a better position to consider her next moves.

In any event, the REBT therapist would actively contest Jenny's belief that she could be rated "a failure". To class herself a failure, Jenny would have to fail at everything. This would clearly be nonsense. The most that could be said is that she might have failed in this particular task. The distinction between who we are and what we do is an important one. Jenny would be encouraged to recognize herself for who she is—a unique, complex, and fallible being who, like all of us, may be skilful in some things and in others less so.

The counsellor would also explore Jenny's subconscious belief that it is necessary to be approved of to maintain her self-esteem. The concept of "self-esteem" seems on the face of it very understandable. If, for example, one individual were to treat another in a very off-hand manner, the person on the receiving end may take it as evidence that he can't be worth much and his self-esteem will take a knock. Indeed, clients often report low self-esteem as the reason for their seeking counselling. But the problem with self-esteem, or self-rating (which is effectively what it is), is that it is largely dependent on other people to keep it stoked up.

So, had the audience been rapturous in their approval that opening night, Jenny's self-esteem would probably have soared. But then how does she keep it up? If, on the basis of her success, she is offered the chance to direct the next play, it is quite possible she will feel anxious all over again, realizing that if she doesn't achieve the positive results she got first time around, down will go her self-esteem. Rather than risk this happening, she might even decide not to direct another production—a pity, because there could, at the very least, be opportunities for her to benefit from her first experience. So she would be losing out all around: denying herself something she might enjoy doing, and feeding a belief that other people's inferred views are a direct indication of her worth. Jenny thus risks finding herself, like the Red Queen in *Alice's Adventures in Wonderland*, running faster and faster just to stay in the same place, as she seeks to meet the unrelenting demands of succeeding and being approved of.

In the place of trying to prop up "self-esteem", REBT encourages unconditional self-acceptance. An important aspect of self-acceptance is making a clear distinction between who we are and what we do, to rate our actions, rather than ourselves. So whilst we might, on occasion, recognize our behaviour as being kind or unkind, or judge that we have done something well or not so well, we cannot from this apply a single evaluation to ourselves, or anyone else, as a kind or unkind person, or one who is good or bad, clever or stupid.

REBT argues that if we accept ourselves unconditionally, then we are in a position to make a dispassionate assessment of our strengths and weak-nesses and assume responsibility for our emotions and behaviour rather than letting them be the product of pressure from outside. This, in turn, enables us to recognize that other people do not have the power to make us feel anything without our assent. The statement "What he said made me angry" can logically be replaced with "I made myself angry about what he said". This acknowledges that emotional responsibility rests firmly with the owner of the emotion. Someone may do their utmost to flatter or annoy us or press our buttons in other ways, but it is up to us how we respond.

It is perfectly reasonable to be annoyed if someone treats us discourteously, or to feel disappointment if we don't achieve a particular goal. It is important that we do have goals as we are probably happiest when we are pursuing an objective that may improve our skills and self-knowledge. A desire to achieve something can be expressed in the strongest terms, as in:

> "I passionately want to succeed in this enterprise, but (and this is the essential qualifier) it would be illogical to insist that I do. There are too many imponderables—my own inexperience, outside factors I couldn't have anticipated, and the necessary involvement of other people. That said, I'll do my very best to make it happen."

If she does not demand success, however hard she works at achieving it, Jenny is more likely to take the risk of making mistakes with her next production and learning from them to achieve her aim of becoming

an accomplished theatrical director. She factors in th
she might fail, but as Woody Allen puts it: "If you're not
failing every now and again, it's a sign you're not doing
anything very innovative."

Ellis devised a very useful format to enable us to
analyse how our thinking may be affecting our emotions and behaviour. He called this "The ABC", and it
breaks down as follows:

A is the activating event

This is what starts things off. The A can be an actual
happening, but it can also be a thought about something that might happen or has happened in the past.

B is the belief

The Belief is our evaluation of the activating event and
how it will impact upon us. In REBT, a belief is designated rational if it is flexible, tolerant, and consistent
with reality, and irrational if it results in our making
rigid demands of ourselves, others, or life in general,
so leaving us with no room to manoeuvre. Our beliefs,
in turn, give rise to:

C—the consequential emotion and behaviour

The outcomes of our beliefs: how we feel and what
we do.

REBT holds that it is not enough simply to reduce an
unhealthy negative emotion, such as anxiety or depression, as the irrational belief from which it stems will still
be there. Clearly, any negative event is likely to lead to
a negative emotion and it would be unrealistic to expect
otherwise. But Ellis wanted to distinguish healthy negative emotions that are the product of rational beliefs

from unhealthy ones arising from irrational beliefs. Feelings which he categorized as the consequences of irrational beliefs are those likely to lead to unproductive and self-defeating behaviour. If we are anxious, we are liable to overestimate a problem and underestimate our ability to cope. In consequence, we may take extreme measures to protect ourselves. The depressed person will tend to see everything in a negative light and may withdraw into themselves. If we experience guilt or shame we are likely to have convinced ourselves we are bad people deserving condemnation, and behave accordingly.

Rational beliefs, according to REBT, sponsor healthy negative emotions. So the recognition of a problem ahead that may prove difficult to deal with may be a cause for concern, but a feeling of concern, as opposed to anxiety, derives from reviewing a potentially threatening situation realistically so that it does not overwhelm us. If, in the wake of a broken relationship or a failure to achieve a goal, we can retain a sense of proportion, we will be sad, rather than depressed, and can still see hope for the future. Remorse is considered the healthy alternative to guilt, and shame is replaced by regret, in recognition that as fallible human beings we don't always succeed in conducting ourselves as we would wish. With unconditional self-acceptance comes the ability to face up to our failings and learn from experience.

Healthy negative emotions are not weak alternatives to unhealthy ones. We may be greatly concerned, extremely sad, or very remorseful, without succumbing to irrational beliefs. But a word of caution at this point. Counselling is rightly described as a "talking therapy", as it is through language that we can share detailed understanding and successfully communicate subtleties of thoughts and emotions. English, having liberally helped itself in its development to a wide range of other languages, both ancient and modern, is particularly fertile in this regard. A generous vocabulary means that any word may carry with it a range of synonyms with subtle variations in meaning.

Counsellors therefore need to ensure that their interpretations match those of their clients. Words like "anxiety", "anger", "envy", "guilt", and "shame" do not necessarily hold the same meaning for everyone. At the time of writing, there has been a lengthy and sometimes heated debate on one of the leading psychology websites as to the precise definition of "self-esteem". Is it the same as "self-concept"? Is it an assessment of personal values? A form of narcissism? The debate goes on.

It is natural to assume that when our friends and peers understand us, others will too, and thus we risk as counsellors resorting to words or constructions that our clients do not fully comprehend and may feel too embarrassed to seek clarification. As discussed in Chapter Four, reflection is an effective counselling technique in which therapists reflect back to their clients the words they used when describing a difficulty or their reaction to a situation. This has the benefit of ensuring that the language stays in the clients' domain. But also, when they hear their words played back, clients may recognize that they have unwittingly presented a distorted picture and may modify their words and thinking accordingly.

We will come to further considerations of language in the following chapter. Meanwhile, for the intending counsellor, "The ABC" is a very useful device for self-analysis. We often cannot change an activating event, but only we have the authority to decide how we will respond to it. It isn't helpful simply to tell ourselves, or anyone else, to pull ourselves together, or stop feeling anxious, or to not get depressed, as according to REBT, our emotions will always be a reflection of our beliefs.

Kate, whose marriage broke up some years back, comes for counselling because she is becoming increasingly anxious whenever the phone rings, so much so she now doesn't answer it but lets callers leave a message, although they don't always do so. The A, the Activating event, is thus that the phone rings, and the C, the Consequential emotion, is that Kate feels anxious. But as there is nothing intrinsically anxious-making about a phone call, the counsellor probes further.

Counsellor: What if you were to answer it?
      Kate: It might be Owen. He's my son.
Counsellor: And if it were?
      Kate: He'll want to borrow some more money.
Counsellor: And if he did?
      Kate: He knows I'm a soft touch. And he won't pay it back.
Counsellor: Why would you have to lend him money?
      Kate: Well, I'm his mother, aren't I.

This has now brought us to the critical aspect of the A, that which actually starts the process off, which is "My son may ask me for money". The emotional C is that Kate feels anxious and the behavioural C is that she won't pick up the phone. But her son asking for money is not intrinsically a cause for anxiety. Parents are often pestered by their children for money, but not everyone will feel like Kate. So what is the B that is driving Kate's anxiety? She reveals her belief is that if Owen asks for money, she *must*, as *a* good mother, give it to him, even though Owen is twenty-two years of age and is in a reasonable job.

The counsellor and the client will now work together to assess the rationality of this belief. Kate comes to see that it is the demands she makes of herself and her son that are the problem. Whilst it would be greatly preferable if Owen did not keep asking for money, there is no law or logic which states that Owen must not do so. Nor must she acquiesce to his demands. Indeed, it can be argued she is doing her son no favours allowing him to be dependent on her.

But two other As emerge at this point, leading to automatic thoughts or beliefs that have previously been unrecognized and each fostering its own B and C. The first A is that if Kate stops giving him money, Owen might break off contact with her. Her belief is that if he did, it would be unbearable, as she is on her own. Her consequential emotion is again one of anxiety, and also of guilt if she should allow this to happen.

Owen tends to spend his money on frivolous things and will sometimes use scare tactics, telling his mother he hasn't enough to pay his portion of the rent for the flat he shares with two others. This leads to a second A: that Owen might end up with nowhere to live. If this happened, her friends and neighbours might think Kate a bad mother. Her belief here is that if they did so, they would be right. This B brings with it a C of shame but also some anger that her son should have put her in this position.

In accordance with REBT practice, the therapist would deal with these issues one at a time to avoid confusion. He would first have Kate consider, for the time being, that these events could actually happen. So Owen does get chucked out of his flat, and he does break off communication. This may sound unnecessarily alarmist as it is unlikely that Owen would mismanage his finances so badly or that he would break off contact with his mother. But having faced up to these worst-case scenarios, Kate is in a much better position to confront them.

The therapist would then encourage Kate to recognize that whilst she might find it very painful refusing to give Owen further money, the short-term discomfort caused would be well offset by the long-term gain of fostering a more responsible relationship with him. Kate may see the logic of this, although she may rather doubt that she could put it into practice. But at this stage, the important thing is for counsellor and client to agree that an alternative way of thinking is valid and that the emotional and behavioural conse-quences will be beneficial.

So, whilst it would be very unfortunate if her son decided to cut himself off for any reason, this would be his decision and tough though it might be, Kate could tolerate it. Better that, than believing she would be so devastated she must never fail to meet her son's demands. With such a belief, she could find herself giv-ing away house and home with no certainty that this would be sufficient. Indeed, it might well encourage Owen to be a bully. Kate agrees that she has the author-ity to deal with the loss, if it occurred, in her own way.

The second A was that people might think badly of her if her son's inability to pay his share of the rent rendered him homeless. If this happened, her B was that this would be proof that she was a bad mother. But even if they did think badly of her on this account, she could not be labelled "a bad mother" as she would have to be a bad mother in all respects and at all times, which would clearly be absurd. But, in taking respon-sibility for her own actions, she may need to acknowl-edge that she has been overindulgent with her son so that he looked to her to deal with his problems rather than resolving them for himself.

Although Kate may intellectually accept these more liberating ways of thinking, it is unlikely that this in itself will be sufficient. The movement from head to heart needs to be driven by a process of vigorous and energetic disputing of her irrational beliefs. As with CBT, this will involve agreed homework assignments designed to encourage her to put into practice what she has learned in the sessions. So Kate and the therapist might agree that next time Owen asks for money she will ask him first to repay her previous loan. She won't enjoy doing this, but the therapist will help her recognize that she is exchanging short-term discomfort for long-term gain. She may move on from this by limiting what she will lend him or requiring her son to produce evidence of a real need. Kate will have always to be aware of her particular tendencies, but knowing what these are will mean that she can intervene before they have a chance to obstruct her rational response to a situation.

It can be seen that REBT is quite a structured and directive approach to counselling and it may seem a bit relentless in pursuing its objectives. It is primarily concerned with the here and now and past events are factored in only where the client may be carrying forward unproductive ways of thinking acquired in earlier years.

Ellis held that counsellors should not be overly warm with their clients in order to avoid the risk of dependency. But he was a great believer in the restorative value of humour, holding that being able to share a joke with the client can do much to cement the therapeutic alliance. This does not, of course, mean the therapist mocking the client but sharing with him or her an element of their work together in a light-hearted way, perhaps recognition of the impossible consequences of a fixed and unhelpful belief.

Ellis is the third practitioner to feature in the series of films *Three Approaches to Psychotherapy.* In this sequence, Gloria tells him of the difficulties she is experiencing finding a new partner. She worries that she is never going to be good enough for the kind of man she would like to be with, so tends to sabotage opportunities to form a relationship by acting in ways that are not a reflection of her true self. Ellis points out that she is seeking the impossible goal of being perfect. Rather as did Carl Rogers, he urges her to accept herself for who she is rather than basing her self-worth on other people's inferred opinions. In this way, she can be genuine, and has a much better chance of finding someone who will like her for who she is. Ellis's very active-directive approach focuses on only the presenting problem, although with more time he may well have explored the beliefs that Gloria may be bringing with her from her earlier life experiences.

CBT and REBT share many features. Both seek the active participation of the client, and both recognize the impact on emotions and behaviour of distorted thinking and interpretations. Both set homework assignments to enable clients to practice recognizing their automatic thoughts or irrational beliefs and taking action to deal with them. There are still fierce arguments, some aired routinely on the Internet, about which is the better, but CBT is the current favoured approach in the National Health Service. Unlike Ellis, Beck kept extensive records of every aspect of his clients' presentations which allowed him to devise questionnaires for patients designed to facilitate the diagnosis of anxiety and depression and identify their needs and vulnerabilities. These inventories have proved very reliable and enable counsellors to work to agreed diagnostic criteria across the board.

This UK state preference for CBT as an evidence-based therapy has angered practitioners of other modalities who feel their approaches are at least as valid and are being arbitrarily discounted. It can be argued that the objectors have a point. Not everyone is suited to the same therapeutic approach; there is no case for a policy of "one-size-fits-all". In practice, a number of counsellors advertise themselves as "eclectic", which simply means that although they may have been trained in one modality they will adapt their approach and draw from others to meet their clients' needs. As you will probably have already recognized, despite their apparent differences, all approaches draw on common themes. All therapists recognize the importance of childhood experience. Few would take issue with Rogers' core conditions of empathy, genuineness, and unconditional positive regard, however they practice. Counsellors who are aware of the impact of conditioning, who have an understanding of the games we play, who have acquired the skills to practice techniques such as Gestalt two-chair method, and who recognize the benefits of out-of-session activities, bring to their practices valuable diagnostic and therapeutic tools. An appreciation of the impact of automatic thoughts and irrational beliefs and methods of addressing these is an important part of their armamentarium.

If you would like to know more about CBT and REBT, Aaron Beck's *Cognitive Therapy and the Emotional Disorders* (1975) is a long title for a very readable book which explores the whole concept of CBT in a lucid and coherent way.

What Is Rational Emotive Behaviour Therapy? (1997) co-authored by three leading authorities in REBT, Windy Dryden, Jack Gordon, and Michael Neenan is a short, clear guide to the theory and practice of REBT. Windy Dryden, who is Professor of Counselling at Goldsmith's College, University of London has also written an instructive pocket book called *A Positive Thought for Every Day* (1999). In this he draws on the philosophy of REBT to set out 365 "thoughts and reflections to sustain psychological health". The content is brisk and forthright but also thought-provoking in the best sense.

With the exception of Beck, all the pioneers of psychotherapy whose life and work we have reviewed so far have now departed, although Albert Ellis, who passed away in 2007, lived to ninety-four. So, what is their legacy and how do advances in medicine and the social climate impact on counselling practice today? We'll explore this in the following chapter.

The counselling environment today

When Freud practised, all his patients were women, all were hysterics, and all were subjected to psychoanalysis or free association. Throughout the history of psychotherapy, individual approaches have often been modified or combined to enhance results or to reflect the pressures of modern living.

For example, Person-Based Cognitive Therapy or PBCT combines CBT with Rogerian perspectives together with the concept of "mindfulness", which lays particular emphasis on immediate experience. In this respect, it shares a platform with Gestalt in which, you will recall, clients are encouraged to concentrate on their feelings, thoughts, and emotions as they experience them in session. Cognitive Analytical Therapy (CAT) is another collaborative approach which combines psychodynamic practice with Kelly's personal construct theory and cognitive-behavioural techniques. Dyadic Developmental Psychotherapy (DDP) draws on the work of John Bowlby to help families whose children have detachment problems, whilst Parent—Child Interaction Therapy (PCIT) integrates behavioural and play modalities to improve parent—child relationships.

But, as so often in the past, some new approaches get a rough ride from the establishment. Neuro-Linguistic Programming (NLP), developed in the mid-1970s, claims to "re-program conscious and subconscious beliefs". But NLP has been fiercely criticized in some quarters as being unscientific and lacking supporting evidence.

Other modalities appear to go right back to pre-Freudian days. Reiki practitioners assert that they can draw upon the energy of the universe to increase their own energy while performing hands-on healing. Thought Field Therapy (TFT) claims to heal a variety of mental and physical ailments through specialized "tapping" with the fingers at specific points on the upper body. Then there is Past Life Regression, which uses hypnosis to reveal memories of previous lives or incarnations. Angel Therapists believe they facilitate healing by helping their clients get in touch with angels who will guide them in the right direction. There is even Abduction Therapy to help those who have been whisked off for examination by creatures from outer space to recover from their ordeal. Magnet Therapy is a thriving business, as are Dolphin-assisted and Flower therapies.

Not surprisingly, authoritative organizations tend to be sniffy about the scientific basis for some of these approaches. The vast majority of counselling is still practised using the methods described in earlier chapters, but the more unconventional approaches are testimony to the powers of suggestion and the often unpredictable nature of the human psyche. As with Franz Mesmer and Phineas Quimby, all the protagonists have their followers who will testify to the effectiveness of their therapies.

Some techniques have been developed to provide support for conditions that have been better understood only relatively recently. "Shell shock", a form of total nervous breakdown brought about by the huge stress of being subjected to heavy artillery bombardment, was initially identified at the start of World War I. However, the army often refused to acknowledge it, accusing affected soldiers of malingering and sending them back to the front where some committed suicide.

Shell shock is now recognized as an example of Post-traumatic Stress Disorder (PTSD) in which a life-threatening experience, such as an assault or being victim of a violent crime, may result in the person suffering intrusive images, sounds, thoughts, or feelings that are linked back to the event. PTSD has generated its own therapeutic approach, Eye Movement Desensitization and Reprocessing (EMDR). This is a still evolving technique, which uses repeated eye movements to activate opposite sides of the brain. This has been found to release emotional experiences that had previously been trapped, so making them accessible to therapy.

The ability of the mind to find unusual ways of representing problems can muddy the water in the counselling environment. As mentioned in Chapter One, Medically Unexplained Symptoms (MUS), the label for any physical malfunction that resists conventional diagnosis, is an increasing occurrence where repressed emotions are experienced as physical symptoms. You may recall Josef Breuer's work with Anna O, also featured in Chapter One. Anna O suffered variously from distortions of vision, headaches, and paralysis, which Freud believed were the direct result of repressed grief over her father's death.

Sometimes such symptoms can defy any attempt to isolate them. I am reminded of a case where a client mentioned the difficulties his grandmother was experiencing with lower back pain. Neither X-rays nor Magnetic Resonance Imaging (MRI) scans revealed anything that could account for this. Eventually, she was given an epidural injection that completely blocked all neural output from the area. Far from being relieved, the patient announced, apparently with some satisfaction, that the pain was as bad as ever! But equally, a condition that may be well recognized in one society may simply not exist in another. In the UK, whiplash injuries are often diagnosed following car accidents and can be disabling for long periods. But a study in Lithuania,[1] where whiplash is unknown, has shown that no one there ever develops it.

Depression and anxiety may be linked with vague physical symptoms such as breathing problems, sleeplessness, headaches, dizziness, joint pain, and migraines, which may need to be taken into account when making an counselling assessment.

* * *

Medicines are another factor that can sometimes complicate the work of the therapist today. With a better understanding of the nervous system and the way that drugs achieve their action, there has been a growing tendency to treat mental ill health with medication. Benzodiazepines and selective serotonin reuptake inhibitors help to relieve the symptoms of anxiety and depression by disrupting the neural pathways that bring about these conditions. But these agents have their downside; they are active compounds that can induce a range of side effects. Some people may remain on them long after the recommended period of treatment, making withdrawal extremely difficult. Children who are behaviorally troublesome are increasingly prescribed drugs such as Ritalin® to bring them under control. But this too has its cost. Common side effects include rash, insomnia, dizziness, nausea, and palpitations.

Then there are the so-called "recreational" substances. The relatively easy availability of cannabis and cocaine (Bolivian Marching Powder to the aficionados) makes it quite likely that younger clients in particular will have experimented with them, and some, unaware of the long-term effects, may have continued using them for some time. The recreational drug world ducks and weaves to keep its "membership" exclusive and no substance of any status is referred to by its chemical designation. So it can be useful to know that "skunk" and "weed" are not synonyms for cannabis, but much stronger and more dangerous concoctions of it. If a young client looks you in the eye (to see how savvy you are) and states that she "just loves miaow-miaow", it's as well to be aware that this has no relation to her feelings for little Tiddles, but refers to mephedrone, a synthetic stimulant presently licensed as a plant food. There are moves to ban it, but this is a very difficult area, because as soon as one substance gets prohibited, other so-called designer drugs are created by chemistry entrepreneurs to take their place.

Some legitimate drugs, so-called "smart pills", have been hi-jacked by students believing they will improve their memory and concentration and so help them get through exams. Often the users have little understanding that these agents can actually cause difficulties with concentration, as well as induce in them anxiety and paranoia and cause memory loss.

It can readily be appreciated that drugs of any kind can adversely affect the therapeutic process.

Alcoholism, too, may sometimes be a problem. That said, it is unlikely in the normal way that the counsellor will meet extreme cases of alcohol or drug abuse, as there are organizations that specialize in helping those with severe addictions.

* * *

You may recall from Chapter Five, mention of the *Diagnostic and Statistical Manual of Mental Disorders* (*DSM*), which sets out standard criteria for the classification of mental disorders. The current version is now being updated, giving rise to a raft of new psychiatric nominations, some of which might seem designed specifically to excuse poor performance and/or bad behaviour. So the child or adolescent who has temper tantrums, a disregard for authority, and a tendency to blame others for their behaviour, can now be classified as suffering from ODD—Oppositional Defiant Disorder, or perhaps Temper Dysregulation Disorder (TDD). But adults needn't feel left out. The man (it is mostly men) who has a habit of flying into an uncontrolled rage at the smallest excuse has an IED—hopefully not the real thing, given his tendency to detonate without warning, but Intermittent Explosive Disorder. And if you find it perversely stimulating to be appalled by pornography or other obscenities you clearly have "Mary Whitehouse Syndrome"—and, no, I didn't make that up, although I doubt it will appear in quite that form in the official literature.

Although the counsellor may not be confronted with some of the more esoteric complexes, the impact of some dysfunctional conditions is becoming increasingly recognized. These may well emerge in the client history and it is important to be informed about them. Autistic Spectrum Disorder (ASD), which impacts on affected individuals to varying degrees, is manifested by a range of emotional difficulties including poor social skills and troubles with language. A portrayal of a form of this disorder, Asperger's Syndrome, is brilliantly evoked in the 2003 novel by Mark Haddon *The Curious Incident of the Dog in the Night-time.* Adults with Asperger's may not be able to see another person's point of view, have poor emotional control, and become anxious if their routines are interrupted. According to the National Autistic Society, over 500,000 people in the UK suffer from autism.[2]

The effects of bipolar disorder, once known as manic depression, are also now better understood. Bipolar disorder can bring with it mood swings which can seriously confuse the counselling work if it goes unrecognized. Paradoxically, dyslexia, although a common condition, is often still undetected, causing misery for those affected where no allowance is made for the difficulties they experience in spelling, reading, and writing. This, too, can cause difficulties for the counsellor if it is not identified.

It can be seen that mental health is an extremely active area and an essential part of counsellors' ongoing work is CPD—continuing professional development—through workshops and seminars designed to help them maintain their skills, learn about new techniques, and keep abreast with advances in psychiatric medicine.

* * *

Psychotherapy and psychiatry, like all other professions, have their own languages, reflected in the abundance of acronyms and shorthand to identify psychological states and therapeutic approaches. These can occasionally be taxing, even for the trained counsellor. For the client who may never have fully articulated their feelings even to themselves, let alone tried to explain them to a third party, finding the right words to explain a way of behaviour that is troubling them can be extremely difficult. Very often such a client may start a sentence with, "I know this must sound daft, but ..." or interrupt the flow of their speech with an anxious, "Sorry, does that make sense?"

The ability to use non-technical language that encourages the client to feel confident and understood and helps them express themselves without embarrassment is therefore crucial to establishing a productive counselling relationship. Partly this can be achieved by being very aware of the client's vocabulary, style of expression, and choice of phrase and, without obviously imitating it, staying within that framework. Metaphors can be very helpful in counselling as they may enable the client to share common ground with the therapist. Encouraging graphic descriptions of mood can help to give substance and colour to what might otherwise be a bare statement. Asking "How angry were you?" and getting the reply "Very angry" doesn't tell the counsellor much. Asking "How would you describe your anger?" and getting the response "I was a pressure cooker trying not to explode" indicates that there may also be an element of anxiety that could be an issue to discuss.

Some metaphors can be more extended. For example, a counsellor might suggest to a client that the process of working through the issues he wants to resolve is akin to weeding a garden. Some weeds may be removed relatively easily, but others are more resistant and involve some hard work to get them out. The satisfaction lies in finally extracting them and exposing the long tap root that has held them in place. A valid adjunct is that as the weeds are removed, the healthy plants have the space and freedom to grow. A metaphor like this can be continued with a humorous touch throughout therapy: "How's the weeding been going?" "I think I've nearly uprooted some we talked about earlier, but there's one that's still proving tough." "Right! Let's get on our gardening gloves!" Metaphors can equally relate the counselling process to a journey of discovery or illustrate the need to persevere to achieve a goal, not unlike the salmon leaping up a waterfall to reach the calmer waters above.

Another form of metaphor is the use of physical symbols—dolls, small objects, models, and pebbles—with different sizes and surface textures. A shelf of items like this may help a client who has difficulty in finding words to describe a mental state. This was the case with Andrea who picked out a Chinese doll with its feet tightly bound. This represented to her the extremely restricted upbringing she had had where her nervous parents would never let her be on her own or take risks. In later years she had few life skills and was forever trying to make herself inconspicuous to avoid confrontations, real or imaginary, which she felt she would be unable to handle. It is somewhat a matter of luck whether a client can relate to a particular object, but this one item, with its distinct image, enabled Andrea to access a complex interaction of beliefs and feelings.

Some therapists undertake training to go a stage further and deploy sand trays in their therapy: miniature sets with props and models through which a client can be helped to set up a world corresponding to his or her inner state.

* * *

The conventions, rules, morals, and attitudes of a culture inevitably impact on the counselling environment and the nature of clients' concerns. In many ways, we live in a quite constrictive society. We are told that the last government created no less than 4,289 new laws—one for every day they were in office. (You disturb a pack of eggs, when directed not to by an authorized officer, at your peril!) A consequence of this frenzy of legislation is that people may inadvertently find themselves with a criminal record—distressing enough in itself. The increasing use of police checks as a prerequisite for employment in a range of occupations can mean that a convicted person, or even someone arrested without being charged, may be unable to follow his or her career path, and the corresponding distress will sometimes present in counselling.

The prevalence of social networking often brings with it an urgent need for acceptance, and failure to achieve this may be seen in the counselling room. Body dysmorphic disorder (BDD), for example, is associated with excessive anxiety about perceived imperfections in one's physical features, while gelotophobia, a fear of being laughed at, leads to those affected isolating themselves to avoid any situation where they may be mocked.

Meanwhile, political correctness dogs even the most innocuous expressions. As extreme examples, when the chairman of a voluntary health watchdog used the expression "jungle drums" in a public meeting to describe the spread of gossip, his remark was seized upon by an equality campaigner on the grounds that it was racist and the watchdog's funding was withdrawn (although it was later restored). An MP who talked of "getting down to the nitty-gritty" during a speech at a Police Federation Conference was reprimanded as the term "nitty-gritty" is banned because of race relations laws. (For the uninitiated, "nitty-gritty" supposedly describes the detritus left at the bottom of slave ships once they had been cleared, although its origin is disputed.)

To complicate matters further, there is the endless parade of euphemisms to avoid any words or expressions that could be deemed offensive and which can create pitfalls for the unwary. The problem with euphemisms is that the new word or phrase quickly assumes the mantle of the one it has ousted so it has to be changed again. The phrase "special needs" designed to replace harsher descriptions like "mentally handicapped" and "sub-normal" has itself now become a pejorative description of someone who doesn't fit in with a particular sub-culture. Likewise, "disabled" has moved through "physically challenged" to the present preferred phrasing of "differently abled". In practice, the innocent use of proscribed words or phrases in the counselling room is unlikely to cause offence, but it is as well to be aware of the connotations such terms can carry.

On top of all of this are the general pressures of living in a computer age, particularly the feeling of isolation that many people experience. We live in a time of entitlement and some will bear a grudge against society or the government if they feel they are being deprived of their rights. According to one study,[3] self-harm is one of the five leading causes of acute medical admission for men and women who have cut or injured themselves as they attempt to obtain relief from the intensity of their emotions.

We may look back over our seemingly secure and free childhood and conclude that we live in alarmingly troubled times, but every period of history has been pretty bad for some people, and often for many. On the plus side, we are not at war, there is no rationing, and we are not in thrall to plague or pestilence; overall, we are probably healthier and we live longer.

* * *

There is no doubt that the practice of counselling brings with it pressures and challenges. It can be frustrating when clients seem not to be making progress, disappointing when our skills fall short of what we feel are needed, and humbling when someone comes to us having managed to cope with obstacles in life which we may wonder how we would have survived. But the work is always engaging and thought-provoking; time and again it provides for the therapist the opportunity to increase their understanding of the workings of the human psyche, and so continue their own development. And there can be few events more rewarding than enabling an individual who may previously have felt trapped to develop the means of moving forward to a more fulfilling life.

Notes

1. Ferrari, R., Kwan, O. & Russel, A. (1999). The best approach to the problem of whiplash? One ticket to Lithuania please! *Clinical and Experimental Rheumatology*, *17(3)*: 321–326.
2. Baird, G. et al. (2006). Prevalence of disorders of the autism spectrum in a population cohort of children in South Thames: The Special Needs and Autism Project (SNAP). *The Lancet*, *368(9531)*: 210–215.
3. Wilhelm, K., Schneiden, V. & Kotze, B. (2000). Selecting your options: A pilot study of short interventions with patients who deliberately self-harm. *Australasian Psychiatry 8(4)*: 349–354.

CONCLUSION

I hope this book has been helpful in enabling you to decide whether to invest in the training to become a counsellor. If you do, there are a few points worth restating.

Accept yourself for who you are

This does not at all mean being complacent, but recognizing that, as humans, we are fallible and imperfect. We have our individual strengths and weaknesses, some situations which we manage well and others less so. We may see abilities in other people we believe we do not have ourselves, but without question these are countered by skills and resources we have developed and they may not. A recent study[1] showed that more than 84% of counsellors in training withheld information from their supervisors because they were fearful of disclosing aspects of their personal life which they feared would elicit criticism. This is a pity. Without the freedom of self-acceptance we become inflexible in our thinking and deprive ourselves of the opportunity to acknowledge mistakes and learn from them or be open about where we may need help to reach our goals.

Thoroughly explore yourself

You need to be very aware of why you want to take up this profession. Use this book to draw on the experiences of those who first contributed to this field to decide how you might want to practice. This is not just a matter of thinking about where your skills might lie, but taking into consideration your natural inclinations and temperament, and drawing on your own background and life experience. This should be done whilst keeping an open mind and with constant reassessment; your training may well throw up a different side to yourself and reveal hidden talents! After gaining your general counselling certificate you will need to invest in two or more years of hard work and thousands of pounds to obtain a diploma in a specific approach. The better informed you are of your skills, interests, and personality, the more likely you will make the best choice and achieve a successful outcome.

Don't take yourself too seriously

Take your counselling seriously, because you are seeking to help people who may be in a vulnerable state of mind, but don't take yourself too seriously. It is right to want to be an effective therapist, but demanding that one be a miracle worker, and that all one's clients should be "cured", can create enormous pressure on the counsellor–client relationship, the more so because such a demand is not realistic. Counselling is by its nature unpredictable. However much empathy and positive regard a client may be offered, all counsellors have successes and failures, all get stuck from time to time, all have clients who fail to turn up or who abruptly pull out of therapy. Such situations are never easy and this is where a good supervisor can be of great help.

Watch out for prejudice

We are none of us as objective as we would like to think. Prejudice against a religion, race, or sexual orientation may be readily detected and can be worked on to be overcome. It's the less obvious intolerance that can cause trouble if it goes unrecognized. Do you have an instinctive aversion to drawling speech, nose rings, lip studs, aftershave, sandals, mauve hair, or tattoos? If prejudices are not recognized and confronted they will intrude into your work and exert a negative influence on the relationship between client and counsellor.

Consider seeing a therapist yourself

Counsellors are probably the better for having been clients themselves at some time, and it can be instructive to explore any personal issues you may have. If you do this, also use the opportunity to study how the counsellor you are seeing works. His style of greeting, attitude, explanation of how he practices, body language, tone of voice, and even how he has arranged the furniture, can all be very informative. It is best to agree to a single session initially and continue only if you are comfortable with the person you selected.

Look after your own needs

If you do take on counselling training and start to see clients, which you will need to do when you study for your diploma, bear in mind that it will be quite demanding, so keep your own well-being in mind. Don't let all your emotional energy be absorbed into your work; spare some for your family, and aim to lead a normal social life.

And a final thought

> The most intense conflicts, if overcome, leave behind a sense of security and calm that is not easily disturbed. It is just these intense conflicts and their conflagration which are needed to produce valuable and lasting results.

—Carl Jung

Note

1. Mehr, K. F., Ladany, N., Grace, I. & Caskie, L. (2010). Trainee non-disclosure in supervision. *Counselling & Psychotherapy, 10(2)*: 103–113.

SUGGESTED READING

Listed below are some books relating to the subject matter in each chapter. All the protagonists of the approaches to psychotherapy wrote extensively about their work, offering opportunities for further reading if you are interested.

Chapter One
Freud: A Very Short Introduction by Anthony Storr
The Freud Reader A Collection of Freud's Writings edited by Peter Gay

Chapter Two
The Interpretation of Dreams by Sigmund Freud
Memories, Dreams, Reflections by Carl Jung

Chapter Three
A Secure Base by John Bowlby
Face to Face with Children: The Life and Work of Clare Winnicott by Joel Kanter

Chapter Four

On Becoming a Person by Carl Rogers
The Carl Rogers Reader edited by Howard Kirschenbaum and Valerie Henderson

Chapter Five

The Psychology of Personal Constructs by George Kelly
The Stories We Live By: Personal Myths and the Making of the Self by Dan P. McAdams

Chapter Six

Games People Play: The Psychology of Human Relationships by Eric Berne
What do You Say After You Say Hello? By Eric Berne

Chapter Seven

Opening Skinner's Box: Great Psychological Experiments of the Twentieth Century by Lauren Slater

Chapter Eight

Cognitive Therapy and the Emotional Disorders by Aaron T. Beck
Mind Over Mood: Change How You Feel by Changing the Way You Think by Christine Padesky
What is Rational Emotive Behaviour Therapy?: A Personal and Practical Guide by Windy Dryden, Jack Gordon, and Michael Neenan
A Positive Thought for Every Day by Windy Dryden

Chapter Nine

The Reason of Things: Living with Philosophy by A. C. Grayling
The Way We Live Now by Anthony Trollope (a satirical novel published in 1875; compare with the present day.)

INDEX